How to garden without a garden: a problem which forms the central theme of this book, and which Xenia Field is best qualified to solve. With the aid of boxes, baskets, tubs and gourds, colourful and impressive displays are possible, and originality should in no way be diminished with space. With a wary and sympathetic eye fixed on budget, Xenia Field gives invaluable advice on choice of seeds and bulbs, dealing with the few necessary skills and tools, and suggesting unusual possibilities such as a choice of herbs or salads to grow.

Xenia Field is the Gardening Editor of the *Daily Mirror*. Her writing on window boxes was her initial passport to journalism, and her powers as a writer on the subject shine as brightly as ever.

Awarded the M.B.E. for services to the Prison Commission, she has been politician, playwright, short story writer and Justice of the Peace; this breadth of experience informs *Window Box Gardening* with wit, originality and style, and an informatively unhackneyed approach.

Fred Streeter: 'It is written in a style that only this author could write – full of detailed information, illustrations and commensense. Here is a book that will help the busy housewife to keep and enjoy her plants' (1st edition). 'I love window boxes and Xenia, so I hope you will read this little book.' (1974)

Window Box Gardening

Xenia Field

Blandford Press London

First published in this edition in 1974
by Blandford Press Ltd,
167 High Holborn, London WC1V 6PH
© Xenia Field 1974
ISBN 0 7137 0656 2

Dedicated
To dear Fred Streeter
by his friend Xenia

Printed in Great Britain by
Unwin Brothers Limited
The Gresham Press, Old Woking, Surrey
A member of the Staples Printing Group

Contents

Acknowledgments

I would like to express my sincere thanks to Victoria Sackville West, whose review of the original edition in *The Observer* sent the book off to a flying start, from which it has never looked back. Also to Mr H. Taylor, O.B.E., for proof-reading and help, to Miss M. Windham who compiled the index, and to Valerie Finnis, who took the colour photographs reproduced in the text and on the cover.

Foreword

Window boxes have played an important part in my life.

In 1949 I went to a Rotarian luncheon, where the guests were invited to unburden themselves to those sitting beside them about their profession or job.

On my right sat a handsome man who lost no time in interviewing me about my work as Junior Whip on the London County Council.

When my turn came to question him he told me he was a publisher. I envied him and said so. He wanted to know the reason.

'Well, it would give me a chance to read more, and I hoped I might write . . .'.

'And what would you write about?' He was a trifle condescending, and had no doubt put the question many times before.

'A book about mayors and their mayoral chains', I suggested. 'So far as I know there is no book on the subject'.

'What else?' The publisher had perked up, his interest aroused by the mayors and their chains of office.

'I would like to write a book about window boxes', I added.

It was a gorgeous early summer day, and I had walked to the luncheon that morning. The sun was powerful, and I had seen hundreds and hundreds of splendid plants wilting and dying of thirst in the well-dressed window boxes of Mayfair and Belgravia. The sun had caught them and had dried them out.

Having been brought up by a gardener, and a gardener myself, I could visualise their tender white roots shrivelling up, some of them burnt against the side of the hot, metal-lined box.

Billy Collins was interested in both books. Which would I like to write first? I chose window boxes: not perhaps such an amusing subject as the dressy mayors, but easier to handle.

Eventually the book was published. 'Bish' Bolam, then the editor of the *Daily Mirror*, read a review copy of my book, liked it and arranged for me to write a Saturday article for his paper.

I was pretty green. I had had two plays produced in the West End and a number of short stories published, but I was no journalist.

Bish's kindly advice was significant. 'I don't mind much if they don't read your article. But if you irritate the readers by including a lot of Latin names and they throw the paper across the room, you will have to go.'

I took that advice to heart and, thanks to window boxes, have spent over twenty happy and rewarding years in the jungle of Fleet Street. Meanwhile, *Window Boxes* inspired John Barralet of Ealing and also London Flowers to start a window-box business.

Barralets now have a garden centre of high standing, a shop and three nurseries to their credit, while London Flowers maintained many of the city boxes belonging to the banks and big business for many years.

1 First Steps

Until the last decade window boxes were as unchanging as the windows themselves. Clearly, there was no scope for a Capability Brown, or the space for drifts of colour, vistas or an intriguing *coup d'oeil*, but there was at least room for more courage and adventure.

Then Constance Spry arrived with her army of flower arrangers, and the window box gardeners caught some of her imaginative spirit. They wanted a change from geranium 'Paul Crampel' and its boring companions, and began trying out different associations with success.

But it is impossible for the gardener to be adventurous unless the nurseryman is adventurous too.

Some nurserymen now take an interest in supplying the gardener with different and more unusual plants suitable for growing on the window-sill, with the result that the scarlet geranium, the Oxford blue lobelia and the white alyssum no longer monopolise the box.

It would be ridiculous to be snobbish about flowers, but when judging window boxes I do get a little weary, not so much of the over-familiar flower faces of trusted favourites, but of the hundreds and hundreds of boxes that look almost exactly the same. We still need more variety in plants and layout. If gardeners would try something a little different and take a chance, they would have more pleasant surprises than disappointments, while there is much to be learnt by the occasional floral flop.

It is surprising how much attention an unusual planting is given by those who walk past.

For many years I grew a box of Black-eyed Susans, *Thunbergia alata*, raised from seed by a country friend with a greenhouse. Their bright orange short-lived blooms, with blackest of centres, came and went day by day, while the pale green foliage climbed up a few small sticks. This plant, too seldom seen, attracted the attention of the passer-by, for the flowers were gay and window box news.

The many new varieties of *Impatiens*, the faithful Busy Lizzie or Patient Lucy, and an attractive planting of little fibrous begonias will captivate an audience in the same way.

There are plants and possibilities for the window box that have not yet been tried, and I hope this book will encourage the gardener to explore new ideas.

Now that so many people have cars and cottages in the country, I make a plea for yet more adventure. With transport, a cottage garden and possibly a greenhouse or frame, the sky is the limit. The flower displays can be changed several times a year when the window boxes are fitted with double, treble or even more trays.

There should no longer be a feeling of guilt in planting the rarer and more expensive conifers for the winter if they can be returned to a country garden for the summer and brought back in the autumn. Bulb trays can be carried off to the country in the late spring to die back at their own pace, not to return to London until they poke their noses through the soil the following year. No longer will there be hesitation in buying the more expensive narcissus beauties such as lovely 'Cantatrice' or, occasionally, 'Salmon Trout'.

Tubs, vases and baskets, which I treat later in this book, further extend the gardener's scope and can be enjoyed by those who have balconies and small paved areas.

I have been writing about window boxes for some years and have no shame in saying that I have changed my mind on certain points in the light of experience. The advice now comes from a better-informed author and replaces a book now out of print and rather out-of-date.

Types of window boxes

There are now window boxes in plenty that should satisfy all tastes and purses.

The fibre-glass box. The newest introduction is the fibre-glass box of eighteenth-century design, the moulds used having been taken from the original boxes.

The box is light in weight, but strong and resistant to weather. Attractive Adam design boxes are to be had from Verine Products.

Among them are the George III box, taken from an original Robert Adam design, the mid-eighteenth-century box that has been in use ever since it was made and the Tudor box featuring the Tudor Rose, *c.* 1500.

A short planter decorated with low relief acanthus and water-leaf pattern has legs and is free-standing; this box will suit almost any window style.

The fibre-glass box is the most decorative box we have and about the most expensive.

The Florentine pottery box. These are of the traditional Italian pink moulded terracotta imported from Florence and are available in different lengths and patterns.

The pottery boxes are extremely pleasant to look at, and I have used them for a number of years. Some are a trifle cramped (only 6 in. deep and 8½ in. wide). I like to have more space and to be able to move on a bedding plant from a 40 pot without disturbing the root ball.

The English pottery box. This is a hand-thrown box by one of the few remaining garden pot makers in the country. I wish the ivy-leaf trough, measuring 2 ft and just the thing for the short window-sill, was easier to come by.

Perhaps I should add that the pottery boxes are vulnerable to very severe frost.

The Minster stone box. Cast in reconstructed stone from the Somerset quarries, the Minster Box is hand finished by master masons and has distinction.

There are several designs: the rock terrace box bearing the simulated marks of the mason's chisel, the plain wall box, and the decorated wall box furnished with a simple design.

Cement and asbestos boxes. These long-lasting boxes have obvious advantages: they are weather resistant, durable and rot-proof.

Florastone, the trade name for boxes made of moulded asbestos cement of a light stone colour, are to be had in three designs: plain, fluted and ripple. Durable, easy to paint and reasonable in price, they are a good buy favoured by the City of London authorities. They are light, washable, frost proof and of the right dimensions.

The plastic box. This box, often described as a ledge-box particularly suited for the small-ledged window-sill, is light and easy to place in problem situations. It is made of rigid polythene or polystyrene. The material is said to retain the heat and therefore to entail less watering, the soil keeping a more constant temperature.

There are a series of different designs with relief decorations, as well as the diamond-patterned and those with simulated white stone finish.

Some suppliers thoughtfully offer window-sill trays to match their boxes (to protect your downstairs neighbour). These are to be had in green, bronze, black and white.

The plastic boxes, reasonable in price, are available at many garden centres and from retail and hardware stores.

The more expensive Verine, terracotta and others can be had in London from the Clifton Nurseries, Maida Vale, Rassells of Earls Court Road and Barralets of Ealing. The gardener should pay one of these firms a visit before making up his mind. Good supplies are usually available in the bigger provincial towns.

The Spanish box. A classical range from Spain of yellow-grey reconstituted stone, a composite of marble, granite, sandstone and other local stones is pleasing, with its high relief carvings, hand finished by a craftsman. Many of them stand on their own feet.

Ammunition box. These unattractive, transitory containers are still seen on occasion, but I cannot recommend them. The metal overheats, absorbs too much heat and plant roots suffer accordingly. The ammunition box, which filled a need after the war, has disappointed many a beginner.

In tropical and warmer countries the tin box may require special insulation to protect plant roots.

The home-made wooden box

The gardener who feels inclined to make the window box himself will have first to choose the wood.

Teak, oak, ash, elm, or deal? I put them in the order of their durability. A teak box will outlive its owner and can be safely bequeathed as a useful if unusual legacy. A deal box deteriorates fast and often dies on its owner, but its length of life is unpredictable. The gardener who believes in buying for dependability will go for the hardwood while the bargain-hunter will be content with the soft timber.

Anyone stationed in the United States will settle for the grand Californian redwood. Should economy be necessary a sturdy packing-case will fill the bill, and will meet all needs while it lasts. If there is a choice of cases, the hardwood should be selected which is at least 1 to 1½ in. thick. Unprotected thin wood is apt to warp.

Making the box. The measurements of the window-ledge will limit the length of the box. If the gardener wishes to lift it in and out, he must allow 2 in. spare either side, so that handles may be attached for that purpose. Handles, that fold flat when not in use, are best put on after the box has been painted.

The do-it-yourself gardener has the advantage of being able to make his box wide and deep so that he can introduce a large plant without disturbing the root ball. I would advise his aiming at a box 3 to 4 ft long, 9 in. deep and 10 in. wide. Length will be determined by the measurement of the window-sill, but if more than 5 ft two boxes will be found more practicable than one. The measurements should allow for the planting of two alternate rows, upright at the back and a second row, possibly of hanging plants tumbling over the rim.

The all-important drainage holes at the bottom of the box can be bored but are best burnt out with a red-hot poker, as charred wood is more resistant to moisture and rot. They should be $\frac{1}{2}$ in. in diameter and about 5 in. apart; they are better placed diagonally than in a straight line or in two alternate rows.

The box should be neatly put together, the wood at the corners dovetailed and brass screws that do not rust employed rather than nails, as they are more reliable.

Sloped wooden wedges fastened to the underside of the box will raise it from the sill and so promote aeration; this will prevent moisture collecting and rotting the wood. The wedges must be deep enough to allow a good flow of air beneath the box or the insertion of a zinc anti-drip tray to catch the inevitable drip.

Attention novices, please! The gardener should examine the wood selected as it is important that the grain should run along the length of the box from left to right and not up and down. It is surprising how many do-it-yourself enthusiasts overlook this most important point.

Drainage. Some growers advise giving the box a slight tilt towards one corner to enable the surplus water to escape to a drainage hole, where the drip is collected by a detachable tin which can be taken off when the water stream dries up. I have seen a number of ugly contraptions, some resembling the innards of an elephant. These gadgets are clumsy and not particularly effective.

If the window or windows are high up and the landlord testy, the gardener is advised to obtain a shallow watertight zinc roofing tray and do his best to remember to empty it before it floods over. A tile tray has the advantage that it absorbs the water, which as it evaporates benefits the plants. Tiles are fragile, however, and a plain metal or fibre-glass tray and a few pebbles serve the same purpose.

Preserving the inside. Once the box is finished it must be treated inside to prevent decay. This is a particularly important operation for softwood.

In the old days I used to advise charring the inside of the box, as some of the wood preservatives were dangerous to young roots. However, this is no longer so and the gardener is perfectly safe in using Green Cuprinol both for his window-boxes and tubs; the salts in the product are insoluble and so are not washed away be rain or watering The solvent must be allowed to evaporate completely, which should take 2–4 weeks or so, before filling the window box.

It is recommended to apply it to the outside as well as the inside. If desired, the outside can be painted over with sealing grade aluminium primer.

Green Cuprinol can be applied by brush, spray or immersion. The manufacturer's instructions must be followed implicitly. A preservative brushed on with care will prolong the life of a box. Re-treatment need only be given at intervals of about five to six years, although it is advisable to inspect window boxes every year and if any cracks have developed to apply a fresh coating, brushing the liquid well into the joints.

In the case of soft wood and those bent on charring their box, the simplest and safest way is to do this work out of doors. Wipe over the inside of the box with paraffin, fill it with newspaper and have a miniature bonfire. The flames can be extinguished by turning the box upside down; a bucket of water, a damp cloth and a sensible helper should be kept handy in case anything goes wrong. Charring can also be done with a red-hot iron or a blow lamp.

Window box linings. There are different schools of thought about linings for boxes. Some gardeners consider that a metal lining is an essential shelter for the protection of roots against a hot sun in a hot street. It retains the moisture in the box and slows the evaporation of water.

On the other hand, the pessimist, sensing a wet summer ahead, prefers the box to dry out between each watering and fears accumulated moisture. When we are foretold the sort of summer to expect, we shall be able to make the right choice.

The advantage of a lining comes in when the gardener has a winter box of desirable small shrubs that he doesn't want to disturb. The lining enables him to lift out the window box shrubbery in the spring and transfer it to the garden, if he has one, until the following autumn. Top-dressed, fed, and pruned into place, the shrubs will come up fresh for a series of years.

Linings can be ordered from the nurseryman or ironmonger in sheet lead or zinc. If the gardener is a handyman, he can buy a piece of zinc of suitable size and fit it in behind the iron panel of the box, not forgetting the drainage. These should last three years or more if looked after.

Decoration. The box should have an undercoat of lead and two or three coats of paint and be re-painted every other year; after that, personal taste comes into play. Green is a general choice, but I prefer white. The townsman may wish to have a gay tile front panel made to hook on and off; the cottager may favour the demure row of palings with a small gateway in the middle. Fortunately, the rustic and cork facing décor, a convenient rest centre for earwigs, has had its day if it ever had one. The choice of decoration should depend on the façade of the house, but the plainer the better.

Security. Decorative window-boxes are an embellishment; safe ones an obligation. In other people's interests, as well as your own, it is vital, especially above ground-floor level, to prevent the box from falling off the sill. It should be attached to the window-frame by a hook-and-eye arrangement; if there are handles at either end it may be necessary to use a short chain to connect the two fittings. Alternatively, the box may be cemented to the wall.

Quite a number of boxes are to be seen hung below the window-sill; and this is the only way of fitting boxes to the new houses and flats that have outward opening casement windows and no sill. Brackets can be obtained or made at the ironmongers to enable them to hang in this way; they are best fitted by a skilled man. This method has two advantages: it facilitates gardening and does not deprive the room of light; the disadvantage is that it is almost impossible to stop the drip.

2   *Soil, Tools and a Warning*

Earth may give the novice the impression that it is a dead substance, when on the contrary it is seething with life and a mass of minute organisms. The population of the window box is greater than that of metropolitan London! The inhabitants in their millions are actively improving soil fertility.

The chemists assist the gardener by providing him with fertilisers that convert alkalines into acids and acids into alkalines, but the experienced gardener contributes as much as anybody to the well-being of the bacteria by looking after the condition of his soil, ensuring that every plant has an attractive root run.

Soil

A good soil compost is vital, and a substantial layer of damp peat over the roughage at the bottom of the box a life-saver. It draws the roots down and holds the essential moisture, preventing clogging.

There are usually a number of different plants in a box and it may be impossible to please the individual requirements of each one. The gardener must do his best to supply a good all-round compost that will satisfy the needs of the majority. Dwellers in big cities seldom have the opportunity of collecting such necessary soil components as coarse river or bank sand and manure, but 'composted manures' in small bags are now freely advertised in the gardening press. In any case, manure must be well decayed before it is put near plant roots: otherwise, it will 'burn' them.

Suitable window box soil is not always easy to come by in a town and generally entails a visit to a nursery, sundriesman, or florist. It seems that most gardeners buy the compost known as John Innes No 2. This is quite in order provided the essential layer of *at least* $1\frac{1}{2}$ in. goes in first.

John Innes composts are carefully balanced proven mixtures containing all the essential plant foods in exactly the right amounts.

Here is the basic mixture of all John Innes Potting Composts:

7 parts, by bulk, of damp sterilised loam (top spit, turves, that have been stacked grass downwards until well rotted).

3 parts, by bulk, damp garden peat: horticultural grade peat must be used.

2 parts, by bulk, of coarse, sharp and gritty sand.

These ingredients are thoroughly mixed together.

To make John Innes Potting Compost No 2, add to each bushel of the basic mixture:

1½ oz of ground chalk. Blackboard, whiting or ground limestone will do.

8 oz of John Innes Base. The base is made up of:

2 parts hoof and horn, ½ in. grist.

2 parts superphosphate of lime.

1 part sulphate of potash.

The John Innes recipe is for the do-it-yourself gardener who appreciates formulae. Others will do better, and very likely come off more cheaply, by buying JIP2 already mixed. Buy no more than is needed for immediate use, as the compost loses its perfect balance, becoming more acid, after three months keeping. The average window box needs 56 lb of compost. Go to the best possible merchant; John Innes compost is not a proprietary product, and many shops sell inferior compost under this name. It is a formula devised by the famous horticultural research institute. Anyone can make it. Your guarantee is not in the name but in the reputation of the shop where you buy it.

The countryman should find no real difficulty in providing a desirable soil for his window box: such as 3 parts rich fibrous loam, 1 part decayed leaf-mould in nice flaky condition, or peat, and ½ part dried cow manure. A 5-in. flower pot of bonemeal added to each bushel of the compost completes a reliable diet agreeable to most plants.

I should stress the fact that straight loam, or ordinary garden soil, seldom gets the best results.

Lastly, soil must be kept sweet and open by constant forking. Learn to recognise soil condition by the look and feel of it. A good compost is capable of retaining moisture and yet crumbles in the hand; if the mixture is clammy or sticky it will cake and pack down on the roots, making it impossible to keep the box properly aerated. Try to keep the soil porous and springy.

Tired soil. Examining other people's window boxes is an excellent way of gathering experience. It will be found that in the majority of cases the soil is completely played out. There is no nourishment left and no substance to which the rootlets can cling. Here, at best, a plant can give an inferior performance; one gets out of the ground only what has been put into it, and I should remind the gardener that some diseases and pests survive in the soil year after year.

London and other large town soils suffer from atmospheric pollution. The gardener living in a dirty area should change the soil in his box every year. In a clean area, however, John Innes can be left in the box for two or three years, provided fertilisers are used correctly and the soil turned over and aerated. A slightly acid soil should be the aim, and oak and beech leaf mould from the woodlands is a valuable addition.

Note: Soilless culture, sometimes seen in America, using Vermiculite to which water and nutrients are added for feeding by inserted wicks, is not generally practised in Britain.

Crocking. A good drainage system is essential, otherwise the soil will turn sour. For this purpose it is best to use crocks, which are fragments of broken clay flower pots. Place one rather large crock, convex side upwards, over the drainage hole in the bottom of the pot, and cover this with a layer of smaller crocks. If short of large crocks, three concave fragments can be folded over the drainage hole: it is important that all crocks be clean. I notice that town gardeners use broken plates for crocking but pieces of clay are preferable to these, being more arched and less sharp and dangerous.

It is of primary importance that the drainage holes should be kept free and open and, to ensure this, the crocks must be covered with roughage capable of retaining moisture and at the same time preventing the compost clogging up the aperture after watering.

Filling the box

Roughage is present in maiden soil; it is the coarser part of the compost such as the residue after sieving. Inch layers of decayed leaves, sphagnum moss, fibrous peat, or a thin layer of turf with its grass side placed downward will all serve to keep the drainage holes free. Hard-coal cinders enable the excess moisture to drain away, but look out for the sooty drip.

The soil must be prepared and ready in the window box at least a week before planting, giving it time to settle before introducing the plants. It is easier to fix the window box before filling it; in any case, the soil should be well mixed before it is put in. A dust-sheet or newspaper should be kept handy when this stage arrives, for filling is a messy business.

The mixed compost should now be put into the box, inch by inch, and carefully pressed down with a flat piece of wood so that the soil is firm all over.

Particular care should be taken that the compost in the corners is as firm as that at the centre, otherwise the water will tear off in all four directions leaving the centre area arid.

The box should be built up in this way until it is filled to within about an inch from the top, allowing a generous space for watering.

Levelling the soil to a flat surface is the final stage; the soil will sink almost imperceptibly in settling.

This is one of the rare occasions when the gardener may knock off for a week or so with an easy conscience, while the soil settles down. But a true gardener watches the soil as carefully as he watches the plants.

Tools

The window box gardener does not require a tool-shed, and the few implements he needs will be a matter of his own preference. All gardeners have their favourite tools. They must include a trowel (for planting) and a pronged implement, possibly a dinner fork (for keeping the soil open), a pair of secateurs or scissors (for pruning), a syringe, a potting-stick or dibble (for planting seedlings), a sharp knife and penknife, a small pair of tweezers (for thinning out seedlings), and a watering can fitted with a rose. Finally, a basket should be handy for the sake of tidiness.

Warning

Living cheek by jowl with a cat-fancier is not advised.

I am constantly being asked for advice on garden protection from dogs, cats and birds. There is a new dog and cat repellent in the form of an impregnated cord known as DCR. The cord is placed 4 to 6 in. above ground level, and tests, it is said, have shown this repellent effective in keeping dogs, cats, rabbits, foxes and other types of animals away. A whiff of another product, Curb, serves the same purpose.

I have smelt the cord and although I did not have the opportunity of testing animal behaviour, there was no doubt about the effect it had on me!

If a neighbouring cat has taken a particular fancy to one of your plants, a few sharp twigs or an unfriendly cushion of gorse will discourage the intruder.

There are various bird repellent sprays but rain washes them off and the birds are soon back again. Nothing is better than a few strands of *black* cotton stretched between twigs a few inches above the plants.

3   The Budget

I never like giving prices of plants, but it is only fair to let the gardener have some sort of idea what his window box is likely to cost him to keep filled with plants, after the initial cost of the box itself.

The nurseryman is as bedevilled as the industrialist by labour and transport problems, added to which he has to contend with uncertain weather. A late frost can be an expensive matter and part of the cost is inevitably passed on to the buyer. Prices will fluctuate, so that this chapter can be but a rough guide. Those that I give are London prices: they are likely to be lower in the country. But a deciding factor in the price is the time spent on the work and the cost of labour involved.

At the florist's

The majority of window box owners concentrate both energy and money on the summer box: geraniums, heliotrope, petunias or other bedders, annuals or half-hardies.

The charge for labour involved in delivery, planting and throwing away tired soil is often surprisingly heavy. Many nurseries prefer to take the boxes back to the nursery for planting.

Petunias or other annuals are a cheaper planting than geraniums, but it appears the majority of gardeners are not prepared to wait for the seedlings to mature and demand an immediate display. A nurseryman tells me that many of his clients have a programme of two or three boxes a year while big businesses may have as many as eight changes. One nursery recommended a cottage-type planting of mixed plants: double daisies, verbena, verbella – quite a gay mixture.

The winter box. This is the most expensive box, but it should be remembered that it can last from October to April. One planted with hebes (veronicas), berry-bearing or variegated shrubs, interplanted with daffodils of the 'Golden Harvest' class would cost about £5. Hyacinths, being more expensive than daffodils or tulips, would increase the price.

The spring box. Auriculas, forget-me-nots, polyanthus, *Primula denticulata* (the drum-stick primula), the claret-coloured primula 'Wanda', and others make a delightful April-to-May spring box, but a luxury one; the winter box can be tidied up and kept presentable until it is time to plant the summer bedding. Here big business has two gay alternatives: double East Lothian stocks or Japanese azaleas. Of these, *Rhododendron obtusum*, a dwarf evergreen shrub, is particularly bright and madly profuse. Such a box will last up to three weeks.

At the nursery

The gardener who plants his own window box and wishes to buy something out of the ordinary run must go to a nursery garden and make his purchase. A visit to a nursery is usually more economical than buying through a catalogue; there are bargains to be had on the spot, and the gardener has the opportunity of selecting a well-shaped, healthy plant from a collection and gets better value for his money. The bigger and better the nursery garden centre, the wider the choice.

Many of the best perennials, if not the newest varieties, are to be had cheaply. The gardener can plant his box to suit his pocket.

Markets, stores and shops

This is the hunting ground for the bedder, annual and seedling. Sturdy young plants are to be had quite reasonably. Geraniums and heliotrope and some of the larger plants are from 40p each. It may be that the gardener will have to decide whether to buy two small geraniums or one large one at double the price. Personally, I am in favour of the well-rooted larger plant; it can usually be relied upon to give a better performance than the two smaller ones put together. Seedlings such as antirrhinums, China asters, and marigolds are to be had at 6–10p each or on occasion as cheap as 40p a dozen. Seedlings that are pot-grown are always a few pence dearer and worth it. Glorious pansies are among my favourites.

Annuals can be bought by the box at a slight reduction. The roots can then be teased out carefully at leisure and a pound well spent will keep a window box and matching tubs gay for two months, short of a hurricane!

Budget figures for a single box

Around £2–4 a year. If this is the limit he can spare, the gardener should concentrate on his spring show and the less expensive bulbs, such as the daffodils

King Alfred and Golden Harvest with scillas, followed by annuals from seed for the summer, such as nasturtiums, candytuft or virginia stock. He must forgo a winter box.

If the gardener spends perhaps 18p. on half a dozen double-nosed daffodils, and say 25p. on yellow crocus, he can still purchase three geraniums and fill up his summer box with petunia seedlings. Any money lef over might be spent on trailing lobelia for the corners of the box. Begonia tubers may be preferred to geraniums. China aster seedlings can always be bought later in the season to fill an ugly gap.

Interesting bulbs can be bought at 30–50p. a dozen and interplanted with polyanthus. The summer box may be planted with the more expensive and less-seen ivy geraniums in different colours, or with fuchsias.

Or the gardener might prefer to spend less on his bulbs and geraniums and to have a winter box of veronicas.

About £5–6 a year. This gardener can indulge in a two-season planting, He can afford a spring box of hyacinths and polyanthus or double daisies. followed in summer by petunias or a block planting of lobelia. In the autumn the bulbs can be interplanted with dwarf cypresses.

Or the gardener may prefer to have a summer planting of cinerarias, succeeded by chrysanthemums, followed by a late winter box of veronicas.

Over £6 a year. The £6-a-year man can let himself go. His bulbs should be top-size and distinguished. His summer show of begonias may include a few named varieties, or hydrangeas could be afforded. An autumn planting of chrysanthemums may be fitted in before the box is planted up for the winter either with small pyramid box, dwarf cypresses or junipers.

It is all too easy for a gardener to spend money. Many of the new varieties and rare plants are tempting and expensive. If funds are not exhausted, the more distinguished daffodil bulbs and begonia tubers are a sure way of depleting them.

4 *Planting*

This is where green fingers come in. I have met people who, through indifference or make-up, are by nature lethal to all forms of plant life. In spite of this, considerate planting and transplanting can be learnt and fingers and thumb trained to be more understanding.

Make a plan. Flower relationships, in the place of counting sheep, is an excellent exercise for anyone who happens to be suffering from a bout of sleeplessness. To conjure up a window box of flowers immaculate in growth and bloom, in brilliant patterns, can be helpful in lulling one to sleep.

A window box should be designed, and it is within your power to make the blossoms blend or clash. Not all flowers look best side by side, and it is for you to decide whether to bring the rival reds together or to keep them discreetly apart.

The time to plant. Autumn, September or October, are ideal planting months in the country, for the earth is still warm and friable. But London is a place apart: plants should come to the cities in the spring, except for bulbs and evergreens for the winter box, which should always be planted in October or November.

Preparation for planting in the garden. All plants should be generously watered the evening before planting out. This greatly simplifies tipping out soil and roots intact.

Planting from pots. Carefully examine every plant before planting. If in pots, they can be removed by inverting them, holding the pot firmly between the fingers of the right hand and supporting the plant with the palm of the left hand, and then tapping the rim of the pot on a table. If the root ball does not respond the plant should be tapped again until it drops out like a sea-sand castle from a child's pail. This shape is known as the gardener's pudding. The root ball should be disturbed as little as possible and the crocks at the base removed by gently disentangling them, while shaking off any loose or dreary-looking soil.

This is the moment to cut off damaged roots with a sharp knife and if necessary to trim the top growth. If such trimming is delayed until after planting the roots are liable to be jerked and loosened from their new moorings. Should the root-ball be found excessively dry it must be soaked in a pail of water for half an hour before being planted.

A hole a little larger than the root ball should have been prepared. If in doubt as to the right depth for planting, study the soil mark on the stem and plant up to that level. Plants have a habit of sinking to a slightly lower level than the beginner expects, and allowance must be made accordingly.

The position that will show the plant off to the best advantage has now to be found. Then, while the stem is held in one hand the soil can be drawn in by the other and firmly pressed down. This firmness round the roots is important and should be uniform. Avoid planting tight, for 'packed' soil is a danger. It is said that a rose cannot be too solidly planted. I have doubts about this. I have seen many roses uncomfortably placed drooping pathetically; in any case, they are not as tender as the annuals.

Loose plants. Plants that are not in pots, among them gifts from the country, arrive loose, and, being unprotected, their roots are particularly vulnerable. They may also be younger stock and therefore more tender. Roots can either be spread out or dropped vertically in the prepared hole; discover by inspection which is the plant's natural way of growth. If the roots are twisted they should be gently unravelled.

Seedlings. Small plants and seedlings can be put in with a 'dibber', but care must be taken that the root drops to the bottom of the cavity and rests on a firm soil bed. Many a wretched plant wilts away, suspended in air!

Distances of planting. Good spacing between the plants is important; every plant must have light and air. On the other hand, there is something in the Irish gardener's remark, 'Seeds grow best when they hear each other growing.' Maybe plants do too.

The distances left between the plants must depend upon their habits, their vigour and the expectation of their growth. Pot plants and bedders may be spaced 12 or 15 in. apart, seedlings not less than 9 in. apart, seeds according to the direction on the packet and bulbs as close as you like so long as they do not touch one another. Three to 4 in. should be allowed between rows (placed alternately).

Careful handling. Plants are fragile. A rough, hasty gesture can seldom be made good afterwards, and successful planting means careful handling. The novice will require practice to become proficient; transplanting is an art. Plants moved in comfort are quick to show their appreciation.

After planting a generous drink may be given, and perhaps taken by the gardener.

5 Bulbs

It is difficult to go wrong with bulbs (and do not forget to water them regularly as they develop), if you buy wisely. The embryo flower will be present in the centre of the hyacinth bulb when you buy it and is protected with fleshy scales against misadventure. If the gardener behaves reasonably, the bulb will flower. If the embryo bloom is not tucked up inside the bulb when it is planted, even the most expert and solicitous of gardeners will not be able to induce a flower.

Bulbs are deservedly popular, dependable and rewarding. They are the city gardener's most profitable investment. Mainly natives of the woods, and therefore accustomed to shady surroundings, they manage with a minimum of sunshine. Their haste in performing before the trees break into leaf brings them into bloom earlier than other flowers, making them all the more welcome.

Fortunately for us, bulbs are tough customers. They rely on their own storeroom for nourishment and can afford to be indifferent to surroundings, climate, and, within limits, to human interference.

The bulb and the corm. A true bulb such as the hyacinth is a form of underground stem that, given congenial conditions, will usually increase in size the following year. A corm lives for one season only and is replaced by young ones that have derived part of their strength from their parent. The crocus demonstrates the corm's manner of growth.

How to buy. Bulbs can be bought from a nurseryman, a shop, market or by catalogue. I recommend buying at the beginning of the season from a well-known firm; specialists have a reputation to keep and, therefore, have their stock meticulously examined for density and soundness. The initial outlay will be a trifle more but the ultimate result far more satisfactory. Many of the big firms ask their purchasers to examine the bulbs on arrival and in the event of any cause for complaint wish to be informed immediately. Paper bags in which bulbs arrive should be opened without delay, so as to provide ventilation.

Some window box owners club together and place a collective order with the nurseryman. The firm is usually prepared to label each bag separately, making distribution easy, and there is a considerable reduction of price on the larger order.

With regard to the quality, I prefer the medium size to the top-sized bulb. The outsize, expensive and fat, often produces two medium-sized flowers, less perfect than if there had been but one, strength and energy having been divided. It is comparatively easy to pick out good bulbs: they should be firm and weighty, not soft and spongy.

Planting and care. The window box must be well crocked, and then filled in the ordinary way with a good soil: two parts loam, one part leaf-mould, a small content of sand, and a final thin top layer of sand, is a suitable mixture. Bulbs should never be brought into direct contact with manure.

When the box is ready for planting, the bulbs can be placed in position on the surface soil. The distances and depths for planting are given under the particular bulb headings.

When perennial plants, such as arabis or aubrieta, are to be grown as a carpeting in between the bulbs, it is advisable to put them in first. Should it be the intention to introduce spring bedding when the winter is over, a space of 8 to 10 in. may be left for wallflowers, forget-me-nots, polyanthus or others.

A trowel is the best implement for planting the large bulbs; a flat-bottomed dibber is more suitable for the small ones, or fingers will do. The surface sand trickles down the aperture as it is made and will help to make a well-drained bed for the bulb. Care must be taken that the bulb sits securely at the bottom of the hole and not on an air pocket halfway down it.

The soil can be pressed firmly around the bulb, but the novice must beware of packing it down too tightly for a pleasant root run. Once the bulbs are planted water may be freely given.

The city gardener is required to use his fork more frequently than the countryman, and on this occasion it is important to keep the top soil free and open. Once active growth is begun the bulbs should be watered two or three times a week, if there is no rain, and never allowed to get dry. Beware of the fast-drying spring winds. Later, as the flower truss appears, and in dry weather, they may need a drink every day, preferably in the evening. Bulbsmen tell me that 95 per cent of bulb failures are due to lack of regular watering. Faulty drainage is also responsible for casualties.

For treatment after flowering see page 56.

Spare trays. Bulb fans often use spare trays; they should leave the plant's foliage loose (rather than knotted, for tidiness), and remove the trays o a shady place outdoors. The leaves will then die back at their own pace while the bulbs slowly ripen.

In late August or September the bulbs can be turned out of the box, fresh soil introduced and the bulbs re-planted, and the growing cycle re-started.

The bulb trays are buried (plunged) in the garden over the winter and given much the same treatment as spring bulbs in bowls grown for the house.

A list of useful bulbs

Those that follow are all suitable for window-boxes. A wider scope still is offered by growing in tubs, for which see Chapter 18.

Aconite. The winter-blooming buttercup, the *Eranthis*, is a tuberous rhizome. It has an engaging Toby green collar and breaks its way through the earth in January. The aconite is the first yellow flower to bloom, and because of its charm deserves a place in the permanent window box where it can stay undisturbed. It is content in the shade, being accustomed to growing under trees.

SPECIES: *Eranthis cilicica.* 5 in. Large golden flowers; and *E. tubergeniana.* 6 in. Large flowers, sweetly scented.

CULTURE. Plant in September or October. They thrive on a horticultural peat mixture that retains the moisture. Depth, 2–3 in. Distance, 2 in. apart.

Autumn-flowering crocus. The autumn-flowering crocuses bloom in September and October. There is something outstandingly attractive about them with their suggestion of spring in the autumn. They should not be confused with the so-called 'autumn' crocus, which is the *Colchicum* or Meadow Saffron.

The average height of the true autumn crocus is 3 in. and there are a number of interesting bulbs besides those named below.

SPECIES AND VARIETIES:

Crocus longiflorus. Lavender with scarlet stigma.
C. salzmannii. Lavender blue with grass-like leaves. Declared to be the best of the autumn-flowering crocuses. Not easy to come by.
C. speciosus. Bright blue goblets with orange stigma.
C. zonatus. Lavender. Particularly hardy.
Bulb growers offer small collections, ten each of five varieties, that give a gay performance just when flowers are becoming scarce.

CULTURE. The autumn-flowering crocuses are content with an ordinary leaf-mould mixture. Plant in late July or August, preferably in a permanent box. Depth, 3–4 in. Distance, 2 in. apart.

Chionodoxa. This pretty little bulbous perennial, 'Glory of the Snow', is an early spring flower of gorgeous blue. It makes a perfect edging for the front of a window box, and is at its best in March. If left undisturbed it will flower for several years, even in London, provided the box is watered until the bulbs have died down.

SPECIES AND VARIETIES:

Chionodoxa luciliae. 6–9 in. Brilliant blue with a white centre. The most popular member of the family.

C. l. alba. 6–9 in. The white form; rare.

C. l. gigantea. 6 in. Lavender blue with a snow-white centre.

C. l. rosea. 6–9 in. Pale rose to lilac, charming, but small.

C. sardensis. 6 in. A true gentian blue, with rather smaller flowers but the best variety. The first blue of the year.

CULTURE. A good ordinary leaf-mould mixture will suit this bulb. It may be planted from the end of August until the beginning of November. Depth, 3 in. Distance, 2 in. apart.

Crocus (spring flowerers). Both the small species and the large hybrids do well in the window-box, and are greatly prized by the townsman. He usually limits himself to one species; as a result his crocus season is a short one. Study the catalogues and attempt a succession of bloom. Crocuses are extremely good value for money, and a large choice is offered. 'Queen of the Blues' and 'Remembrance' have led the field for the last thirty years.

HYBRID VARIETIES:

'Joan of Arc'. A magnificent white with bright orange stigma.

'Queen of the Blues'. Soft lavender with purple shading at the base and wonderful texture. A free flowerer.

'Remembrance'. Purple-blue. Often described as the best crocus under cultivation.

'Striped Beauty'. Lilac striped with a purple base. A splendid bicolour.

'Yellow Giant'. Golden yellow; large flowers. A cheerful character.

These flower in March. Height 3 in.

SPECIES:

Crocus biflorus. Cream, with outer petals feathered deep purple. Early March.

C. chrysanthus 'Moonlight'. Chrome yellow fading to cream. January-March.

C. c. 'Snowbunting'. Cream feathered indigo, with a yellow base and deep orange stigma. January–March.

C. c. 'E. A. Bowles'. Buttercup yellow. An outstanding member of the section. January–March.

C. imperati. Inner petals violet, outer petals fawn feathered deep violet; scented. December–March. Often the first to flower. Height, 4 in.

C. purpurea grandiflora. Purple.

C. susianus (Cloth of Gold). Rich golden. February–March.

C. tomasinianus. Lavender. March.

C. t. 'Whitewell Purple'. Reddish-purple. March.

These are particularly recommended for the rockery window box. Collections of fifty of these bulbs (ten of each of five species) are offered by the growers – a thoroughly good investment for any permanent box. Height 3 in.

CULTURE. Crocuses may be planted in September with the daffodils or later on with the tulips, but they should be in the ground before the end of October. The corms are strong growers and look after themselves; they are satisfied with any good all-round soil mixture. If the soil is really poor it can be improved by forking in a dressing of horticultural peat.

Planting is best done in clumps of double or treble lines. Should the gardener wish to let his crocuses remain in the window box a second year or more, he must give the leaves an opportunity of dying back. They can be kept tidy by tying them in loose knots. After a year or so the corms work up out of the soil partly as the result of their habit of forming new corms above the old ones. Once out of the soil they should be replanted. Depth, 3 in. Distance, 2–3 in. apart. The corms should not be allowed to get too dry after planting.

Birds attack the crocus and destroy the flowers, but even the London sparrow hesitates before he trespasses upon the window box. However, if need be, the flowers can be protected by a network of black thread.

Daffodil. See under Narcissus.

Fritillaria. This small bulb is the snake's head fritillary or chequered lily. The pendent bell-shaped flowers are rose, lilac, dark purple, and white, and are handsomely spotted. The mottled fritillaria has great fascination, is easy to grow, and blooms from April to May. Height about 12 in.

SPECIES AND VARIETIES:

Fritillaria meleagris alba. Creamy-white on slender stems.

F. m. 'Aphrodite'. Almost white, and strong growing.

F. m. 'Purple King'. The darkest of the family.

A mixed bag will give an interesting variety.

CULTURE. These small bulbs are hypersensitive to the air, and it is therefore unwise to buy them from the shop counter, where, exposed to the atmosphere, they shrivel and perish. Well-conditioned bulbs should be bought from a reputable firm.

Planting should be done in September or October in a good sandy loam; the bulbs require little water but respond to occasional doses of liquid manure before flowering. Fritillaries dislike being transplanted and should be left undisturbed in the permanent box. Depth, 4 in. Distance, 3 in. apart.

Grape hyacinth. The bright blue *Muscari*, that mostly flower in March following close on the heels of the crocus, rarely fail to give a good account of themselves.

SPECIES AND VARIETIES:

Muscari azureum. Cambridge blue. Early February; 6 in.

M. botryoides album. White and scented; 6 in.

M. 'Early Giant'. Indigo-blue; 8 in.

M. 'Heavenly Blue'. Bright sky blue, and unquestionably one of the most beautiful of the grape hyacinths. The flower spikes are stout and the colour vivid. April; 8 in.

M. praecox alba. White, of peerless quality and great beauty. 6 in.

M. comosum plumosum. Mauve, plume-like fascinating, but something of a freak. May; 8 in.

M. racemosum. Navy blue, and the darkest of all; 8 in.

CULTURE. This is another bulbous perennial that, if left undisturbed, will thrive for some years. The bulbs should be planted in September or October in a good leaf-mould soil. Easy to grow, they have no special tastes. Depth, 3 in. Distance, 3 in. apart.

Hyacinth. The hyacinth, with its strong stem and loaded truss of bell-shaped flowers, has always been a favourite in the window box. A formal plant, it fits in particularly well with any symmetrical pattern. Here again the medium sized bulb is recommended for the window box, the outsize being likely to produce a top-heavy spike that will topple over in a wind. For this same raeson the double hyacinth (not to my mind an improved flower) with its weighty truss is best left out. I suggest second size bulbs, specially selected, hand-picked and healthy.

VARIETIES:

'City of Haarlem'. Deep yellow. One of the best.

'Jan Bos'. Red.

'Indigo King'. The darkest of the blues.
'L'Innocence'. Pure white. Strong stem. Very popular.
'Madame du Barry'. Best scented hyacinth. Nearest to red. Medium-sized
  spikes.
'Myosotis'. Light blue. Glorious colour. Large truss.
'Ostara'. Eton blue. The bells are large and of great beauty.
'Pink Pearl'. Clear pink with closely set bells. Short. Sturdy.
'Queen of the Pinks'. Bright pink. Highly scented. A reliable bedder.

These are a few dependable varieties. Blue varieties, such as 'Bismarck' and
'King of the Blues', are favourites commercially, mixing well with daffodils.
They vary little in height, being all some 12–14 in. Season and situation affect
both the time and the duration of the blooming period.

The 'Cynthella' hyacinths, with their graceful loose spikes, are also suitable
for window-boxes, and are to be had in all shades.

CULTURE. An ordinary compost of loam, leaf-mould, peat and sand in equal
proportions is adequate; but the hyacinth likes a certain richness, and, as
organic manure is rarely available, a dose of fish manure is a handy tonic.
This can either be worked in with a fork or sprinkled on the surface of the
soil and watered in.

Planting should not be done in wet weather. Hyacinths are sun-loving
plants that will not tolerate damp, and care must be taken that the soil is neither
wet nor soggy when planting takes place.

Hyacinths may be put in any time between September and December;
most gardening experts advise planting before the end of October. Bulbs
should be put in 4 to 5 in. deep, and spaced about 4 in. apart: a sprinkling of
sand at the bottom of the hole makes an excellent dry bed for the bulb and is a
wise precaution against rot.

A thin covering of straw or layer of leaves during a hard winter will prevent
the foliage from being damaged by frost. If the window box is in a windy
position early staking is essential.

Once active growth has begun the watering-can must be used generously,
the bulb never being allowed to go dry.

Iris. The lordly 'flag' irises that adorn the outdoor garden are not suitable
for window boxes. They grow from a thick, flat, fleshy stem called a rhizome.
Many of them flower late at an awkward moment, just when the gardener
wants to get on with his summer bedding. In addition to this, they are on the
tall side for the window box and renowned for the shortness of their flowering
season. Against this the novice may note that irises of varied species are to be

found in flower almost the whole year through, many of them are easy to grow, they are cheap and of remarkable beauty.

Here is a small selection from four important groups of bulbous irises.

DUTCH:

'Golden Emperor'. Golden yellow; 33 in.

'Imperator'. Lavender purple, strong grower; 27 in.

'Princess Irene'. Pure white standards, deep orange falls. New and much recommended; 14 in.

'Wedgwood'. Pale blue. The first to flower; 22 in.

'White Excelsior'. White, elegant; 22 in.

These flower in late May and early June.

SPANISH:

'Cajanus'. The best yellow.

'King of the Blues'. Rich blue.

'Hercules'. Purple-blue with bronze shading.

The Spanish sweet-scented iris flowers in June, about a fortnight after the Dutch and a fortnight before the English group. Very elegant. They are similar to, but smaller than, the Dutch varieties, growing to about 14 in.

ENGLISH. Less variety in colour in this group and no yellow. Among the best are:

'Coombelands'. Rich Oxford blue. Larger flowers latest to bloom.

'Mauve Queen'. Pinkish-mauve blotched purple.

'Purple King'. The best purple. Large and vigorous.

These flower from late June to July, and require protection from the frost; 1–2 ft.

DWARF SPECIES:

I. danfordiae. Golden yellow. Early February; 3 in. Can be disappointing.

I. histrioides major. Blue with a golden crest. Referred to deservedly by the specialist as a gem. Late January onwards; 4 in.

I. reticulata. Rich violet, blotched yellow. Scented. February; 9 in.

Flowering from January to March, and perfect for rockery compositions or the connoisseur's permanent collection, the dwarf irises present the richest of colours.

CULTURE. The Dutch and the Spanish iris require a well drained light sandy soil; the English section prefer a slightly heavier mixture. The whole family has a taste for fish manure, which may be introduced a week or so before planting is begun.

October is the best month for planting, which should in no case be left later than the middle of November, otherwise the bulbs are inclined to become soft or shrivelled. The Dutch and Spanish should be planted about 3 in. deep and about 6 in. apart, the English an inch deeper but at the same distance apart.

The iris, other than the dwarf species, will be found to be accommodating and prepared to grow anywhere. The dwarf genera are pernickety; they require a warm sheltered position and a gardener's care. The iris is often called the 'poor man's orchid' and it is a pity that more poor men do not grow them.

Narcissus. Narcissus is the correct name for all the different types of daffodil. There is, however, a tendency to call the large yellow trumpets daffodils and the white or pale varieties with small cups narcissi, but we may with perfect propriety call them all daffodils if we wish. Meanwhile, the Royal Horticultural Society has classified the whole genus into eleven divisions.

The daffodil is the city gardener's favourite bulb. Spoken of by Socrates and the Egyptians, it has been cultivated universally for many centuries. The British and Irish hybridists have led the field in its development. The flowers have grown in substance, but I often hear the botanist complain that the modern daff is lacking in refinement. There is keen rivalry between the bulbs, and one variety is quickly superseded by another in the race for size and colour.

The pink cups are growing in importance and the general public are becoming accustomed to the new rose tints and apricots, but the yellow trumpet reigns supreme. There are fashions in daffodils as in other flowers, and just at the moment the pink trumpets are catching the public eye.

I have picked out my list from the superabundance available; most of those named are my own particular favourites, others have been added upon the helpful advice of the bulb specialists. The new and too expensive have been omitted. The revised system of classification, which may appear rather pompous, has been followed not because it is more logical, but for the reason that the bulb salesman is now advertising his bulbs under these new headings.

The large trumpets are perhaps the best class for the window box, but it is pleasant to have a change. Narcissus 'collections' are offered by all the big firms and are worth consideration. There is a great deal of pleasure and experience to be had from twelve bulbs (two each of six varieties, at various prices).

The daffodil flowers in March and April; in the list of the divisions that follows 'early' denotes March and 'late' about April.

DIVISION I. Members of this division have one flower to a stem, and the trumpet or corona is as long as or longer than the perianth. It is subdivided into groups A, B, and C.

Group A (Trumpet and perianth both yellow):

'Golden Harvest'. Golden yellow. The master yellow daffodils at the price. 20 in. Early.

'King Alfred'. Golden yellow. Popular veteran. Cheap. In 1900 the bulbs were priced at £6 each; today they cost 50p upwards for 10 bulbs. 18 in. Early.

'Magnificence'. Deep golden-yellow trumpet. 14 in. Early.

'Rembrandt'. Deep golden-yellow trumpet. 14 in. Late.

Group B (Trumpet yellow, perianth white):

'Queen of the Bicolors'. Creamy white, short yellow trumpet. 16 in. Early.

Group C (Trumpet and perianth both white):

'Beersheba'. A flower of perfect form, with a large flat perianth and a long and superbly flanged white trumpet. The blooms often measure 5 in. across. 21 in. Mid-season.

'Mrs E. H. Krelage'. Snowy white with a cream trumpet. The best, cheapest and sturdies of the whites. 16 in. Late.

DIVISION 2. The large-cupped (or short trumpet) narcissi belongs to this division. There is one flower to a stem and the cup or corona is more than one third but less than equal to the length of the perianth segment. Choices:

'Carbineer'. Flat yellow perianth, large deep orange-red cup. Brilliant. 22 in. Mid-season.

'Carlton'. A clear yellow with a graceful frilled crown, and magnificent bearing. 20 in. Early.

'Mrs R. O. Backhouse'. A white perianth and a large trumpet-shaped crown of pale apricot pink; 20 in. Mid-season.

DIVISION 3. Small cupped, perianth white, corona coloured. Choices:

'La Riante'. White perianth-crown, brilliant orange-red. Very free flowerer. 14 in. Late.

'Verger'. Large white perianth, with lemon yellow crown, bordered orange. 17 in.

DIVISION 4. These are the doubles. Choices:

'Irene Copeland'. A perfect double. Longer petals, creamy-white, shorter ones apricot. 14 in. Mid-season.

'Van Sion'. The favourite double daffodil. Excellent for a windy position. 13 in.

26

DIVISION 5. *N. triandrus* with slightly reflexing petals: 'Liberty Bells', shining lemon, and 'Angel's Tears' beloved by the flower arranger.

DIVISION 6. *N. cyclamineus*: overlapping petals gracefully swept back. Enchanting and among the first to bloom. 'February Gold', robust 10 in., one of the best for window boxes.

DIVISION 7. These are the jonquils including the natural species *N. jonquilla* and many beautiful hybrids. They have more than one bloom on each stem and are sweetly scented.

'Trevithian', several round golden flowers, 15 in., strongly scented, recommended by Michael Jefferson-Brown. Mid-season.

'Jonquilla'. The true single jonquil is gay and elegant, with clusters of small and sweetly scented flowers. 13 in. Late.

'Orange Queen'. Deep, deep orange-gold. Three flowers to a stem. Late.

DIVISION 8. *N. tazetta*, bunch-flowering or polyanthus narcissus. 'Geranium' with 4–6 round flowers, white and rich orange-scarlet is a delight. Very sweet-scented.

DIVISION 9. The *poeticus*, or 'Poet's Narcissus'. These varieties are scented; the well-known 'Pheasant's Eye' is includes in this division.

DIVISION 10. Miniatures and miscellaneous species. These are perfect for the rockery box, but can also be introduced in the forefront of any other composition. A few choices:

N. bulbocodium conspicuus. Small golden flower with a yellow hoop petticoat. Rush-like foliage. 6 in. Early. Not free-flowering first year.

N. cyclamineus. Rich yellow trumpet, with sharply swept-back perianth. Enchanting and among the first to bloom. Enjoys shade. 6 in. Very early.

N. triandrus 'Albus'. The creamy white 'Angel's Tears' daffodil. Exquisite and greatly admired. Slender growth, cluster of elegant, cyclamen-like flowers with globular cups and perianths 7 in. Mid-season.

DIVISION 11. 'Papilion'. A new 'collar' race that departs from the traditional narcissi form. The corona is split and covers more than two thirds of the perianth. 'Parisienne' is a fine example ,with a white perianth and large reflexed and ruffled orange cup. An exciting flower.

CULTURE. The daffodil likes a good, well-drained open loam. It benefits if given a moderate diet of bonemeal or well-rotted stable or cow manure, which, alas, is seldom available in a city. In its absence a dressing of a good organic manure (Eclipse fish manure or hoof and horn) worked into the soil prior to planting, is recommended.

27

So far as planting is concerned it has been stressed for many years, by all and sundry, that the daffodil must be safe in the ground by the second week of September. Gilbert, our gardener, instilled this idea into me at an early age, and no doubt I shall always hasten to plant my daffs as he bade. However, many of the modern growers consider this haste quite unnecessary and declare that no benefit is derived from the early start. They are satisfied that the bulbs are equally well off if they are put in during October.

The majority of gardeners appear to set their daffodils about 4 in. deep, only planting deeper on very light soils. The professional instruction (which I always follow) is to measure the bulb from base to shoulder, and then to plant at double that measurement. Shallow planting is practised to induce early flowering, and the Dutch growers have shown how highly successful this method can be. The bulbs may be planted about 5 in. apart. The spacing will depend largely on the room available, but on no account must the bulbs be allowed to touch each other. They cannot give of their best if overcrowded.

Bulbs may be watered generously when planting is done, after which water should be used sparingly until a sound root structure has been developed.

Scilla. This family is particularly important to many of us, as it includes the English bluebell that is found in the woods in May. The dwarf Squills, that thrive in sun or shade, are enchanting, and bloom from February on.

EARLY SPECIES:

S. bifolia. Cobalt blue. 3 in. Listed in the catalogues as showy. Miniature. The first to flower.

S. sibirica. Oxford blue. 3 in.

S. alba. Pure white, and not quite so sturdy as the blues. 3 in.

S. 'Spring Beauty'. A marvellous colour and the most popular. Twice the size of *S. sibirica*; a good laster of strong upright habit. 6–8 in.

MAY SPECIES (*Scilla campanulata*). These are the taller growing 'bluebells'.

S. hispanica. The robust Spanish Bluebell, light-blue.

S. h. alba. White.

S. h. 'Rose Queen'. Soft lilac-rose.

S. non-scripta. The English bluebell, with arching stems.

S. n. alba. The white form. Superb. One of the most graceful flowers that exist.

Added to this there are several charming campanulata hybrids. These are all 12–14 in. high.

CULTURE. Scillas like a good leaf-mould, and should be planted in late September to October. Plant the little early sorts 3 in. deep and 2–3 in. apart.

The May-flowering scillas should be planted 4 in. deep and about 3 in. apart. They resent being transplanted and are at their best in clumps.

Left undisturbed, these bulbs will flower for some years. The blue scillas mix admirably with tulips.

Snowdrop. The *Galanthus*, the common snowdrop, is usually the first flower to bloom in the window box. It is in every way an uncertain performer and is not an ideal subject for the box. During a warm winter it will flower in February. Like all small bulbs, it looks best in groups.

SPECIES AND VARIETIES:

Galanthus elwesii. Single, large, earliest of all. 8 in.
G. nivalis. The ordinary snowdrop. 6 in.
G. n. flore pleno. The double form. 6 in.
G. n. maximus. Large and vigorous: single. Highly recommended. 8 in.

CULTURE. The snowdrop may be planted in September or October in a good ordinary soil. Depth, 3–4 in. Distance, 2–3 in. apart. It is equally content in the sun or a shady corner, and if left undisturbed will flower for several seasons – if it finds your window box to its liking.

Tulip. The tulip is the most brilliant-coloured bulb of the day, and it stands up to window box conditions as well as, if not better than, other bulbs. A petal may fly off in the wind, but the stem remains stout and firm.

Tulips in their hundreds are divided into a number of sections; there follows a small selection from an enormous list. Here are a few.

EARLY SINGLES:

'Couleur Cardinal'. Rich cardinal-red, long lasting. 13 in.
'De Wet'. Golden orange stippled with orange scarlet. 13 in.
'Ibis'. Deep rose pink, large. 14 in.
'Keizerskroon'. Scarlet, deeply edged with bright yellow. Handsome and the brightest and best-known variety. 14 in.
'Mon Tresor'. Pure yellow, good habit. 12 in.
'Pink Beauty'. Rose with a white flush through the centre of the outer petals. Vigorous. 13 in.
'Van der Neer.' Rich purple-mauve, striking. 12 in.

These bulbs of glorious colour are used largely for garden borders. They do not possess quite the size of bloom or length of stem of the May-flowering varieties, but their sturdiness is an advantage for window box cultivation, and they are easy to grow. The early single begins to flower in late March, and flowers on through April.

'Golden King'. A deep golden. Paeony-shaped.
'Marechal Niel'. Canary yellow, flushed orange.
'Peach Blossom'. Rosy pink. Erect and gay.

These are all 11 in. high. Good for windy positions.

The early doubles appear in April, a little later than the singles; the flowers are larger and more robust than those of the singles and last longer. Nothing is more beautiful than a small collection of these tulips, and they are to be had at a reasonable price. They are the darlings of the nurseryman as they transplant well before flowering (tulips are not good movers). They use 'Orange Nassau', 'Scarlet Vuurbaak' and 'Peach Blossom' with great effect.

LATE DOUBLES. Although biased against double flowers I much admire this group with paeony-like blooms. They are the tulips of the future, possessing great lasting qualities. They arrive a little later than the single tulips and adore the sun. In the wet weather a friendly shake will prevent their becoming heavy with rain. These tulips have new and virile blood. They flower a little late for the geranium and summer bedding enthusiast waiting to plant out. Choices:

'Eros'. Old rose. One of the best doubles ever seen. 24 in.
'Mount Tacoma'. White and green. 20 in.
'Uncle Tom'. Burgundy. Glossy. Great substance. 20 in.

COTTAGE TULIPS. These tulips, like the Darwin, are rather tall for the window box; they give a magnificent display in May. Their symmetrical heads in soft colours are extremely elegant. Choices:

'Mrs John Scheepers'. Clear yellow. Largest bloom of its group. 26 in.
'Marjory Bowen'. Bright salmon pink with orange glow. 28 in.
'Marshal Haig'. Among the most brilliant scarlets. 30 in

TRIUMPH TULIPS. Here is a new race of tulips raised by a Haarlem nurseryman: it is a cross between the single early and the Darwin. These bulbs have remarkably strong stems, a large range of colours and are highly vigorous. They flower in late April and the early weeks of May (some ten days later than the early single). This is a tulip that can stand up to adverse conditions and the exposed position of many a window box. It is the pick of the bunch for the townsman. Choices:

'Bruno Walter'. Chestnut-orange; faint purple bloom. Scented, 20 in.
'Crater'. Rich crimson; dusky outer petals. 18 in.

'Piccadilly'. Cherry red with a white margin. 22 in.
'Princess Beatrix'. Bright red and gold. 24 in.
'Reforma'. Butter yellow.

PARROT TULIPS. The Parrot tulip, the Bohemian branch of the family, with its fascinating laciniated petals, is not entirely reliable in window boxes, and has an unfortunate habit of bending its neck and getting damaged by rain. Sheltered position essential.

A collection of twelve bulbs, two each of Allard Pierson, 'Blue Parrot', 'Fantasy', 'Orange', 'Favourite', 'Red Champion' and 'Sunshine' provide an element of excitement. The Parrots are May flowering.

LILY-FLOWERED TULIPS. The charm of this flower is its reflex petals. They are a cross between the cottage tulip and the Darwin, possessing a strong constitution, and are May flowering. Selections:

'Yellow Marvel'. Deep yellow, 24 in.
'Picotee'. White, edged rose. 24 in.

DARWIN TULIP. The May-flowering Darwins are tulips of stately bearing and rich colour. They are veritable giants in size, and rather too tall for the exposed window-box, but excellent for tubs. Nearly a hundred varieties of Cottage and Darwin tulips are planted in the London parks each year, and are worth the gardener's attention. Selections:

'All Bright'. Dark red. 24 in.
'Bleu Aimable'. Lavender Mauve. 25 in.
'Charles Needham'. Pale scarlet. 24 in.
'Clara Butt'. Pink, first rate. 26 in.
'Golden Harvest'. The best golden yellow. 27 in.
'Ossi Oswalda'. Ivory white splashed cherry rose. Changing colour as it develops. 28 in.
'Pride of Zwanenburg'. Rose pink. 29 in.
'Prunus'. Rose pink with a salmon glow. 30 in.
'Queen of Night'. Velvet maroon black. Wonderful. 30 in.

TULIP SPECIES: For gardeners who are interested in botanical tulips there is a wide field of choice. The flowering season opens in March with cream *T. turkestanica*, 18 in. and closes in June with orange scarlet *T. sprengeri*, very scarce. 18 in. Other good ones:
T. clusiana. 'Lady Tulip', cherry red and white. 8 in. April. Has great charm but requires a warm, sheltered position.

T. fosteriana. Enormous brilliant scarlet blooms with a black or yellow base. 12–15 in. March–April. Very showy and effective but a little tall. Early.

T. f. cantata. Flame, soft buff. 9 in. March. These come in every colour and shade and are superb. They are gradually becoming cheaper – thank goodness!

T. kaufmanniana. The enchanting 'Water-lily tulip', cream and carmine. 6 in. March. Wide-petalled, cone-shaped flowers. There are now several hybrids.

'Madam Lefeber'. (5 in. also called 'Red Emperor'.) Oriental scarlet. Extreme beauty. 15 in.

T. princeps. Oriental scarlet. Also exceptional. 10 in.

T. tarda. Clusters green, purple and white flowers. 3 in.

T. greigii. Give a bright show.

CULTURE. It is generally agreed that October is the best planting month for the tulip. If planted in September there is the danger of the bulb poking up its nose too early and getting nipped by the frost. There is the further risk of disease when the bulb is planted too soon.

The tulip requires a light, rich soil of loam and leaf-mould, and a well-drained window box. The careful gardener plants his tulips in fresh soil each year, so running less risk of disease. It is easier to plant the bulbs with a trowel than a dibber: they should be placed 4 in. deep and about 5 in. apart.

If the tulips are retained for a second year, the flower heads will be much reduced in size, and some of the bulbs may fail to bloom altogether. On the other hand, the old bulbs form one or two bulblets which, if carefully nursed, may flower the following season. Cultivation of the bulblets in the window box is not satisfactory; here, then, is one more gift for a country friend.

In 1962–3 bulbs in many window boxes were damaged by the frost. If we should have such another hard winter the gardener should protect his box as best he can with sacking or some similar protection.

A suggestion. Don Ryder, the knowledgeable manager of Rassells nursery, plants bulbs in three layers in his own window boxes.

Daffodils are laid on the soil at the bottom layer to flower in April.

Golden double tulips 'Van der Hoef', lightly covered with soil, form the second layer.

The third layer of small bulbs are planted in groups and include *Iris reticulata*, scillas and others that do not flower later than mid-April.

6   Flowers from Seeds

Seed growing is the cheapest method of propagation when a number of plants are wanted, and there is the outside chance that one may rear a new and exciting seedling. But growing from seed in a window-box is difficult and experience has taught me that few plants can be raised and relied upon for bloom and colour. Gardeners are better off with inexpensive seedlings.

But I do not wish to give the impression that seed growing in boxes cannot be done. And whatever the outcome, sowing and growing are useful in teaching the novice gardener how nature works.

Soil. A well-broken-down crumbly loam is ideal for seeds, with the top inch finely sieved. But incomparably better for the beginner than this is the John Innes seed compost, which can be had from a florist or nurseryman. Not only does the compost set the seeds off to a galloping start, but it also stops the decay that attacks the hardiest seedlings. Most gardeners have had the sad experience of watching sturdy young plants topple over, suddenly and unexpectedly, just as people flop and faint on a hot day in a crowd. The 'damping-off' fungus is extremely prevalent and deadly among young seedlings. By using compost that has been sterilised, all foreign organisms such as undesirable bacteria and insect eggs, are eliminated. The compost can be bought either by the bushel or in 7-lb bags, or John Innes seed compost will fill the bill.

Sowing. The eager beginner often makes the mistake of sowing too early. February to April sowing is advised in towns; few seedlings have the vitality to survive winter in any big city. It is a good plan to sow seeds of the same kind at slightly different dates to ensure a succession of bloom. However, advice is usually given on the packet.

Seeds may be sown either direct in the window box, in a seed pan or pot, or in a shallow or herring box known as a 'flat'. Whatever the manner decided upon, the drainage must be exemplary. The simplest and the most practical way is to sow direct in the window box, avoiding any move. The advantage of a pot is that it is easy to handle and examine. If only a small quantity of

33

seedlings is wanted, this is an excellent way of getting to know a genus and becoming a gardener. Cleanliness is essential, and the pot must be conscientiously scrubbed.

The grander and more professional way of doing things is to sow in a shallow, flat seed-box. If the gardener wishes to keep a flat permanently by him, it should be of hard wood, $\frac{1}{2}$ in. thick. Otherwise, being in contact with moist soil, it will warp, rot and fall to pieces. The flat should be at least $2\frac{1}{2}$ inches deep, allowing for a substantial layer of drainage material. The slats that go to make the bottom of the box should be spaced at least a quarter of an inch apart so that there is a reliable runaway for excess water. The size is of no particular importance, but small seed containers are lighter and easier to handle. Tne window box gardener rarely needs a flat larger than a cigar-box; if he treats it with safe Cuprinol it will last longer and prevent disease. (See page 5).

When the time comes to sow the seeds, the soil in the flat or box should be pressed down with a piece of board so that it is firm and the surface even. For a pot or small round container the base of a tumbler is suitable. When considering sowing it is worth bearing in mind the well-proven adage: seeds should be covered with their own depth of soil. A little extra covering must be provided if the weather is hot and the box or pot sunbaked. The tendency of the beginner is to sow too thickly and too deep.

To cast seed finely, as is recommended on the packet, is by no means as easy as it sounds and is utterly impossible in a wind. First a corner of the seed packet should be opened and held high and steady, then the seed should be evenly scattered, avoiding any jerky movement that causes the forming of small heaps.

There are those who sow in straight line furrows row by row, and others who practise station sowing. The latter method involves sowing at intervals, in small pinches or heaps which some gardeners say enables them to distinguish more easily between weed and seed.

Very small seeds are a problem to handle; they can be mixed with a little sand before they are scattered, and shaken out of any suitable form of sifter. There are kitchen gadgets that fulfil the purpose. I have used a Ludo dice-shaker with good effect. Small seeds need no covering; some gardeners like to press them down lightly into the surface soil with the board clamp to ensure making them firm.

Large seeds, such as nasturtiums or canary creeper, are sown singly and require deeper sowing; at least twice the depth of their own diameter, and about 9 in. apart.

34

I watched an expert seedsman sowing flats by the score. 'You can't sow too thinly,' he emphasised. 'No two seeds touching'. When the work was completed he covered the seeds lightly with sifted soil. 'I spread this over just like a second sowing', he went on to explain, and his hand made the same smooth movement as in the first operation. There was the same care and concentration, and only a suspicion of a finely sieved dressing for the smaller seeds.

Germination. Seeds germinate more easily in the dark, and those sown direct in the window box can be covered over with a sheet of brown paper or newspaper resting on pegs or pencils and held in place by small stones.

Seeds sown in pots should be covered over with a sheet of glass so that the soil may retain its full moisture. A sheet of paper should be laid on top of the glass. The glass covering may be lifted daily so that any condensation can be wiped away before it causes drip.

Some seeds germinate fast, others slowly. Although few seeds germinate as readily as mustard and cress yet candytuft, Virginia stock, and others will sprout within a week or so. I found auriculas laggard in showing sign of life, but eventually after a couple of months they all came up. Lilies are slower movers, and fritillaries have been known to take a year to germinate. Patience is advisable, especially with gift seed about which little is known. The gardener must be prepared for idiosyncrasies.

Proof of germination is given by faint white sprouts.

Seedlings. After the happy event of sprouting, the paper covering must be removed, as, once started, the seedlings will require plenty of light. In order to acclimatise them to this without too much blinking, the paper shades should be removed at night so that young growth encounters the dawn before the day.

Seedlings that have been kept in the dark too long are easily distinguishable by their drawn-up, anaemic appearance, and the readiness with which they damp off. Once a leggy seedling always a leggy seedling.

The town gardener without a greenhouse, frame or garden can raise easy-going annuals and half-hardies indoors.

I have been particularly successful with the little French marigolds, 'Naughty Marietta' and her colleagues, that seem to enjoy a sunny kitchen window sill provided they get plenty of light and the upper part of the window is opened when the temperature rises above 45–50° F. (7–10° C.)

Seedlings raised in a living room are bound to be underprivileged and should be found a sheltered place on a balcony or outdoors as soon as danger of frost is past.

Ventilation. Ventilation should be increased as the seedlings mature, so that they may harden off gradually. After the seeds have germinated, the glass covering can be lifted an inch or so on warm days and the ventilation gradually increased until the seedlings are accustomed to the air and are hardened off. Any sudden change of temperature should be avoided, but air is essential to plant life and a lack of it has been responsible for many an early demise. Plants, like children, are grievously affected if checked in growth, and have great difficulty in readjusting themselves.

Thinning out. Seedlings grow rapidly and soon need more room in which to develop; overcrowding must be avoided, as this is bad for all concerned.

The seedlings should be transplanted or thinned out.

Large seedlings such as marigolds can often be comfortably lifted within ten days of germination. Small seedlings such as lobelias are better left to grow for about three weeks before handling.

Beginners may care to adopt the safer method of gently pulling out the unwanted and discarding them, although this will result in fewer seedlings. It is certainly a better way when dealing with those that do not recover from the check of transplanting and the cluster-growing annuals such as Virginia stock and linaria that do not transplant satisfactorily.

After thinning out, the firming up of the remaining seedlings may be necessary.

A less rigorous thinning out may be wise should the youngsters cramp their neighbours and rob them of the air and light.

In deciding upon which seedlings to discard, the novice should not throw away all the small seedlings, so long as they are healthy; size has little to do with their future standard of performance. Thinning out should not be done hurriedly if seedlings are to be removed without disturbing their neighbours.

The first leaves to appear on the infant plant are its 'seed-leaves'. Not until then do the true leaves appear. As soon as the first true leaves have fully expanded, the seedling is ready to be lifted out of the flat or pot and transplanted into the window box. Proceed as in Chapter 4 and do not leave it too late.

Later on, pinching out (removing the top of the upright growth) will encourage branching and result in bushy plants and more flowers. This should be done once or at most twice. Otherwise, flowering will be considerably delayed.

Moisture. Moisture is vital to seeds and its importance cannot be over-stressed because without humidity the seeds will not germinate. Once they are sown, watering becomes difficult and there is the risk not only of disturbing the seeds but of washing them away altogether. To prevent this, the soil should be well dampened before sowing so that the seed can absorb the moisture it needs until anchored by its own root structure, when it can stand up to a watering-can. The window box or container should be soaked thoroughly from the start; pots can be stood in pans or saucers of water and left until the moisture rises to the surface of the soil. If this is done, watering will rarely be necessary before the seeds come through, but should the soil become dry before there is sign of sprouting, steps must be taken; the soil must be given a spray with a syringe from above or a gentle watering from a can fitted with a rose.

Once germinated, the seedlings can be watered more generously. It is all important that the soil does not dry out at any stage. Nurserymen soak their seedlings pans in a shallow tank and then lift them out to drain.

Kept 2½–3 in. apart, the seedlings will not come to any harm if left for three to five weeks.

A list of useful seeds

★ Denotes plants more suitable for tubs than window boxes

Annuals

	Colour	Height	Flowering Time
Alyssum	White, violet and pink	4–6 in.	June–Oct.
Calendula (Marigold)	Yellow, orange	12–15 in.	June–Oct.
★*Centaurea* (Cornflower)	Blue, carmine, rose, white	12–36 in.	July–Sept.
★*Convolvulus* (especially the variety Royal Marine)	Blue, white, rose	2–3 ft	June–Sept.
Godetia (dwarf mixed)	Shades of pink, crimson and carmine, blotched and picotty-edged	9–12 in.	July–Oct.
Iberis (Candytuft)	Various	12 in.	July–Aug.
Larkspur	Various	1–4 ft	June–Sept.
Sweet Pea			
'Little Sweetheart'	Various	8 in.	June–Oct.
'Bijou Bush'	Various	15 in.	June–Oct.
Linaria (Toadflax)	Various	6–12 in.	June–Sept.
Linum grandiflorum 'Rubrum' (Flax)	Red	15 in.	June–Sept.
Malcomia (Virginia Stock)	Pink, white	9 in.	May–Sept.
Matthiola (Night-scented stock)	Lilac-mauve	1 ft	June–Aug.

	Colour	Height	Flowering Time
Phacelia campanularia	Blue	9 in.	July–Sept.
Reseda (Mignonette)	Green, yellow	6–12 in.	July–Sept.

Note: Mignonette is tricky but worth trying. Best sown in a pot. Transplants poorly. Later the pot can be sunk in the box.

	Colour	Height	Flowering Time
Tropaeolum (Nasturtium)	Pink, red, orange	12 in.	July–Oct.
T. canariense (Canary Creeper)	Yellow	10 ft	July–Sept.
Viscaria	Various	10 in.	July–Oct.

When possible, dwarf varieties should be chosen.

7 Bedders and Perennials

The market cart loaded with bedding plants of every colour is an enchanting sight. The dazzling effect of these small bedders, pressed tightly together in their boxes, is seldom reproduced to the full in a window box. They are at their best packed close, and it is a luxury to buy a box at a time and keep them intact on a tray. They are, in the main, annuals, and usually half-hardy ones.

Few of these fast-growers are heavily scented so don't miss Cherry Pie variety 'Garfield' – not a showy heliotrope but by far the most sweet-scented.

Plants are classified according to their span of life. The well-known school-boy's howler that 'annuals die once a year, biennials every other year, and perennials last for ever' may be inaccurate, but at least it gives some of the story.

Annuals give a quick return, but they are tired out by the autumn, They are divided into three classes:

Hardy Annuals (e.g. marigold and larkspur, strong and undemanding). Seed can be sown in spring or autumn on the site where it is to bloom; spring is the better period for the city gardener. I have dealt with these in the previous chapter.

Half-hardy Annuals (e.g. ageratum and petunia). They depend on pleasant conditions and the temperature. They must be raised under glass and are planted out in late May or early June. The half-hardy annual seldom lives longer than six months.

Tender Annuals (e.g. nemesia and schizanthus). These require cosseting and must be raised under glass.

Biennials. The biennial takes a second year to accomplish the cycle that the annual performs in one year: it generally flowers during the second year and having played its part, gives a curt farewell. Examples are wallflowers and sweet williams.

Perennials. The perennial lives for an indefinite period, usually years; the majority die down in the autumn, giving the root structure something of a rest, and return in the spring. In fact, there is an annual and miraculous resurrection. They do not strictly fall under the heading of bedders, owing to their performance, and are therefore listed separately at the end of this chapter.

I am often asked to name a plant that flowers the whole year through. The answer is: maybe in heaven; not here!

Buying

What makes a good window box plant?

A tidy habit.

A free flowerer – flowering at least two out of the twelve months, or better still three.

The ideal window box plant does not reach more than 12–18 in. in height.

These three requisites ask a lot and limit the number of desirables. In towns seedling plants can be bought in boxes or pots from a street barrow, at the market stall, in a garden shop or at the local nursery. They can also be ordered by post from a distant nursery.

It is always best to see the plants and pick for oneself. A nursery usually offers the widest selection, but the barrow and the stall often have good stock of the popular and easy lines.

The gardener should choose plants that are well hardened-off – those that have been gradually accustomed to outdoor conditions. They will be the short, bushy ones of the darker green; the lighter green specimens will still have an air of the glass-house or frame about them. If the young plants are unaccustomed to outdoor conditions they may well resent the sudden change of atmosphere when put in the window box and die off.

It is sometimes argued that the gardener is more likely to obtain better stock and named varieties from a distant nurseryman than from the market or street trader. This is probably true, but against this the nursery produce has to stand up to the packing, and however carefully this may be done, a tender young plant is apt to be crushed in the journey. Once damaged it does not recover easily, not possessing the stamina of the shrub or the members of the herbaceous border.

However, several of the plants in the lists that follow may not be obtainable locally and it may be necessary to order them by post.

Planting

Safely home, the plants should be got into the window-box as soon as possible.

If the root balls are parched, they may be soaked for ten minutes in a basin of water, care being taken that the rootlets are not damaged.

Plants should be placed 5 to 12 in. apart, and generously watered after planting. Follow the advice in previous chapters for planting and watering. All being well they will get away without check, oblivious of the change in surroundings.

Culture

Plant life is highly concerned with regeneration and the reproduction of its species. It takes no chances, and flowers at the earliest moment; once the flower is over, the seed will set. This is especially true of the short-lived annuals, hardy or half-hardy. Once the seed pod swells, the plant loses youth and vitality, flowering is slowed (if not halted altogether) and the plant puts all its energy into reproduction. The persistence with which a plant will replace flower after flower, hoping to get away with it, is a valiant struggle to carry on the race and is fascinating to watch. If the gardener fails to step in and cut off the dead head before the seed is formed, the plant wins the day and never flowers wholeheartedly again.

Apart from this watchful deadheading, the bedder has no particular requirements.

A list of useful bedders

* Denotes plants more suitable for tubs than window-boxes

	Colour	Height	Flowering Time
Ageratum	Blue, white	6–12 in.	July–Oct.
Alyssum	White, mauve	2–12 in.	June–Oct.
Antirrhinum (Snapdragon)	Various	12–18 in.	June–Oct.
Begonia (tuberous and fibrous-rooted)	Various	8–12 in.	June–Sept.
Bellis (Daisy)	Red, pink, white	6–8 in.	Apr.–June
Calceolaria	Yellow, brown	12 in.	July–Sept.
Tagetes (Dwarf French Marigolds)	Yellow, orange	6–12 in.	June–Oct.
Callistephus (China Aster)	Various	18 in.	June–Oct.
*Canna (dwarf varieties, full sun)	Crimson, red	2–3 ft	June–Sept.

	Colour	Height	Flowering Time
Celosia (Cock's Comb)	Red, yellow	18 in.	July–Sept.
Chrysanthemum (dwarf varieties)	Various	1–3 ft	July–Oct.
Dianthus chinensis (annual pink including the Hedde-wigii varieties)		9–12 in.	July–Aug.
*Dahlia (dwarf varieties)	Various	18–36 in.	July–Oct.
Fuchsia	Various	1–2 ft	June–Sept.
Geranium (ivy-leaf and zonal varieties)	Various	6–18 in.	June–Sept.
Heliotrope (Cherry-pie	Mauve-purple	1–3 ft	June–Sept.
Impatiens (Busy Lizzie)	Pink, orange, scarlet	6 in.	June–Sept.
Lobelia (especially the trailing sorts)	Blue, red and white	6 in.	Aug.–Sept.
Marguerite (Paris Daisy)	Yellow, white	1–2 ft	June–Sept.
Marigolds (dwarf French)	Yellow, red	4–12 in.	June–Oct.
Matricaria	Yellow, white	12 in.	June–Sept.
Mimulus (Musk)	Various	6 in.	May–Aug.
Myosotis (Forget-me-not)	Blue, white, pink	6 in.	June–July
Nicotiana (dwarf varieties)	White, red	2–3 ft	July–Sept.
Pansy	Various	6 in.	May–July
Pentstemon (annual varieties)	Various	1–2 ft	July–Sept.
Petunia	Blue, pink, red and yellow	12–18 in.	July–Sept.
Phlox drummondii	Pink, red, white	12 in.	July–Sept.
Polyanthus	Various	8 in.	Mar.–Apr.
Salvia (Clary)	Red, blue	2 ft	July–Sept.
Stocks, Ten-Week	Various	12 in.	Apr.–July
Tagetes signata 'Pumila'	Yellow, orange and red	6–10 in.	June–Oct.
Verbena	Various	9 in.	July–Sept.
Viola	Various	6 in.	May–July
Wallflower	Various	12 in.	Mar.–Apr.
*Zinnia	Various	15 in.	July–Sept.

A useful list of perennials

* Denotes plants more suitable for tubs than window boxes
† Denotes half-hardy perennials.

	Colour	Height	Flowering Time
*Anemone japonica (Japanese Wind-flower)	Pink-purple, white	1–3 ft	July–Aug.
*Aquilegia (Columbine)	Various	1–3 ft	May–July
Armeria (Thrift)	Pink, red	2–18 in.	Apr.–June
Aster (Michaelmas Daisy)	Various	1–5 ft	June–Sept.
Dianthus (Carnations and Pinks)	Pink, red, white	6–24 in.	June–Sept.
Doronicum (Leopard's Bane)	Yellow	2–3 ft	Apr.–May
Dracocephalum (Dragon's Head)	Violet	12–18 in.	June–July
Erigeron (Fleabane)	Various	1–2 ft	May–Oct.
Erysimum (Alpine wallflower)	Yellow	1 ft	May–July
Gaillardia	Yellow, bronze	18 in.	June–Oct.
†Gazania (in hot sun)	Red, orange	6–9 in.	June–Oct.
†Geranium (see Pelargonium)			
*Geum (Avens)	Red, orange, yellow	1–2 ft	May–Oct.
Helleborus (Christmas Rose: a deciduous perennial)	White, pink	6–15 in.	Dec.–Apr.
Hesperis (Sweet Rocket)	Various	1–3 ft	June
Heuchera	Red	1–2 ft	June–Aug.
Hieracium (Hawkweed)	Yellow	12–18 in.	June–Aug.
Hypericum calycinum (St John's Wort)	Yellow	1 ft	June–Aug.
Iberis (Candytuft)	White	1–2 ft	May
Mentha (Mint)	Purple, pink	1–2 ft	Aug.–Sept.
Nepeta (Catmint)	Mauve	12–15 in.	May–Oct.
†Pelargonium (Geranium)	Various	1 ft	June–Sept.
*Salvia pratensis (Clary)	Blue	2 ft	June–Aug.
Sedum (Stonecrop)	Various	2–18 in.	Aug.–Oct.
Sisyrinchium	Blue, yellow	1 ft	June–Oct.
Stachys lanata (Lamb's Ears)	Various	1–2 ft	June–Aug.
*Statice (Sea Lavender)	Various	6–24 in.	July–Sept.
Tolmiea menziesii	Green	1 ft	Apr.
Trillium grandiflorum (Wood Lily)	White, pink	1 ft	May–June
*Veronica (Speedwell)	Blue	1–2 ft	June–Sept.

Doronicum, London Pride, St John's Wort, Woodruff, *Tolmiea* and *Trillium* are good for windows on the shady side of the house.

Dwarfs

★ Denotes perennial

Low growing and dwarf forms of annual and herbaceous plants fit comfortably into the limited space of a window box:

	Colour	Height	Flowering Time
Anchusa capensis	Blue	18 in.	July–Oct.
A.c. 'Blue Bird'	Blue	18 in.	July–Oct.
Antirrhinum nanum var. *compactum*	Various	9 in.	June–Oct.
★*Arabis*	Various	4–8 in.	Mar.–June
★*Arenaria montana* (Sandwort)	White	2–6 in.	June
Asperula (Woodruff)	Pink, white	3–8 in.	June–Aug.
★*Aster* (dwarf forms) (Michaelmas Daisy)	Various	9–12 in.	Oct.
★*Aubrieta*	Blue, pink, purple	2–4 in.	Apr.–June
Calendula officinalis (Marigold)	Yellow	12 in.	June–Oct.
★*Campanula*, Rock species	Blue, white	1–4 in.	June–Aug.
Centaurea cyanus (Cornflower)	Various	12 in.	July–Sept.
★*Chiastophyllum oppositifolium*	Golden yellow	6 in.	Apr.–June
★*Chrysanthemum maximum* var. 'Esther Read'	Double white	12 in.	June–Aug.
Corydalis (Fumitory)	Purple, yellow	6–12 in.	May–June
Eschscholzia californica (Californian Poppy)	Various	6 in.	July–Oct.
E. caespitosa	Yellow	6 in.	July–Oct.
Godetia (dwarf varieties)	Various	9 in.	July–Oct.
Gypsophila (dwarf varieties)	Pink	8 in.	July–Sept.
★*Lavandula compacta nana*	Lavender	6–9 in.	June–July
★Lily of the Valley	White	6 in.	May
★*Lysimachia nummularia* (Creeping Jenny)	Yellow	Creeping	June–July
Omphalodes cappadocica	Blue	6 in.	May–June
Petunia (dwarf bedding varieties)	Various	6–12 in.	July–Sept.
Phlox nana compacta	Various	8 in.	July–Aug.
★*Primula auricula* (Dusty Miller)	Various	6 in.	Apr.–May
★*Saxifraga umbrosa* (London Pride)	Pink, white	6–10 in.	May

	Colour	Height	Flowering Time
*Sempervivum (Houseleek)	Pink, yellow	4–12 in.	June–Sept.
*Silene pendula (Catchfly)	Rosy, purple	6–9 in.	July–Aug.
Tagetes signata patula (French Marigold)	Yellow	9 in.	July–Sept.
*Thalictrum minus	Yellow	6–9 in.	June–Aug.
*Thymus (Thyme)	Various	3–12 in.	June–July

8   Pots – An Alternative

Some people have not the time nor, possibly, the inclination to grow their own plants. They may prefer to buy pot plants in bud or in bloom, and to stage a flower display on their window sill. This is an easy way of doing things if money is no object. A faded plant can be whipped out and replaced with a quick buy from the shop round the corner; something in bud or something in flower that will give new life to the ensemble, and the exchange can be made without creating even a minor disturbance.

Mature plants just about to flower are expensive and cost 40–50p a pot. Geraniums will last throughout a season, but other flowers such as yellow daisies or marguerites seldom last more than a month or six weeks. Six or eight pots will be required to fill the sill.

Window display on these lines is expensive, and gardening less than half the fun. However, it provides plenty of colour, and the slightly pot-bound geranium, if well fed, often flowers more profusely as a result of root confinement.

The pots can be stood inside an ordinary window box or a mock window box may be easily fixed with a front panel and two ends.

In both cases the pots should be stood on a tray of pebbles or upon independent saucers in order to avoid drip. If it is desired to give the impression that the plants are growing in the box a top-dressing of moss will complete the illusion.

Pot sizes

When going shopping it is useful to know the size of the pot that is required· Clay pots are made in Standard sizes, with numbers that denote how many the potter made out of one cast. The smaller the size the higher the number; the depth of the pot is approximately the same as its diameter.

72 pot	.	.	2½ in. diameter (Thumbs)
60 ,,	.	.	3 ,,
54 ,,	.	.	4 ,,
48 ,,	.	.	4½–5 ,,
32 ,,	.	.	6 ,,
24 ,,	.	.	8½ ,,
16 ,,	.	.	9½ ,,
12 ,,	.	.	11½ ,,
8 ,,	.	.	12 ,,

Clay pots are cheaper than they were and can be bought by the dozen; the price of a dozen 60s is about 50p.

Many nurserymen favour the plastic pot, and no wonder – no breakages and far less watering involved, as they do not absorb the moisture. But I, and I believe the plants with me, remain loyal to the well-tried clay pot.

Care and culture

The advantage of growing plants in pots is that each plant can be given individual attention. Plants can be balanced in shape by giving them a turnabout every week, so that they get the light from all angles and are not 'drawn' by the sun. During watering each pot can be taken out, plunged in a pail of water and allowed to drain before being returned. This obviates any question of drip.

Pot plants dry out very quickly, and extra care must be taken that they do not get dry. It is a good plan on scorching days to stand each pot in a larger one, otherwise the rootlets that are right up against the hot clay are likely to get damaged. Some gardeners sink their pots in damp peat. In any case pots require more watering than a window box and regular feeds of fertiliser.

This way of doing things has another pull. It is fun to be able to ring the changes, sometimes to concentrate all the blossom on the passer-by and the street, and sometimes to be miserly and steal the colour inside for oneself.

The majority of these summer pot plants are annuals, and once they are over they should be removed from the pot to the dustbin.

Bulbs can be given to country friends, or stored for the following year. (See page 56).

Perennials can be kept if the gardener has room for them. The hardy perennial, such as the chrysanthemum, can remain outdoors on the sill; the half-hardy, including the fuchsia and geranium, must be brought indoors, before the frost.

This sort of window-box gardening seldom holds the gardener's interest for long: he prefers to grow his own plants. He will not rush to the window when he comes in to see what has happened while he has been away. He looks at his plants with a certain pleasure as he might at the florist's window, but he will not experience any of the gardener's joy at seeing a seed sprout or a cutting that has dangled its head for days suddenly stiffen and perk up. These are miracles for the grower only. Although pot-gardening ensures an effective display, it is expensive and gives little scope for the gardener's skill.

Some good pot plants

	Colour	Height	Flowering Time
SPRING POTS			
Daffodils		16 in.	Mar.–Apr.
Grape Hyacinths (*Muscari*)		6 in.	Mar.–Apr.
Hyacinths		8 in.	Apr.–May
Lily of the Valley		6 in.	May
Tulips		12–18 in.	Apr.–May
SUMMER POTS			
Antirrhinums		12–18 in.	June–Oct.
Begonias, large-flowered bulb varieties		9–18 in.	June–Sept.
Begonia semperflorens (fibrous rooted)		6 in.	June–Oct.
Celosia plumosa		18 in.	July–Sept.
Chrysanthemums (annual varieties)		2 ft	Aug.–Oct.
Coleus, brilliant foliage		3 ft	July–Sept.
Fuchsias		2–3 ft	July–Oct.
Gazanias (for a hot window)		6–9 in.	June–Oct.
Geraniums (and Regal Pelargonium)		1–3 ft	June–Sept.
Heliotrope (Cherry Pie)		12–15 in.	June–Sept.
Impatiens (Busy Lizzie)		6 in.	Jan.–Sept.
Kochia ('False Cypress')		2–3 ft	
Marguerites		3 ft	June–Sept.
Mesembryanthemums (for a hot spot)		4–6 in.	July–Sept.
Nasturtiums (*Tropaeolum major* and *T. minor*)			July–Oct.
Nemesias		9 in.	July–Sept.
Petunias		12 in.	July–Sept.
Salpiglossis		2 ft	June–Sept.
Salvias (new pygmies)		15 in.	July–Sept.
Schizanthus		24 in.	Aug.–Sept.
Stocks, Ten-Week		12 in.	Apr.–July
Viscaria (Lychnis)		12 in.	July–Oct.

	Height	Flowering Time
AUTUMN POTS		
Asters (dwarf varieties)	1 ft	June–Sept.
Chrysanthemums	2 ft	Aug.–Oct.

WINTER POTS

Small shrubs make excellent pot plants. (See page 72.)

9 *Everyday Management*

There is no place for the casual labourer in town gardening. The neglected window box can look even more slatternly than the neglected herbaceous border. Care must be earnest and constant, and the gardener must get to know his plants.

Soil aeration. Success is largely determined by a good well-conditioned soil. Surface soil must be kept aerated with a fork; that is to say, kept open otherwise in a short time it becomes unwholesome and unfit for plant habitation. A kitchen fork will do, but every care must be taken that the tender rootlets, which are the plant feeders, are not injured or exposed in the process.

If the soil is of the best and is regularly forked it should remain in fair condition for a year even in London or Manchester. The surface soil may deteriorate in spite of attention, in which case the top inch that is affected, crusted or discoloured, should be removed and replaced with fresh compost. It requires an expert to detect 'sourness', but even the novice can tell when soil ceases to be crumbly and healthy.

The gardener would be wise to make it a rule to change the soil completely at least every second year.

Drainage. The importance of drainage has been stressed in a previous chapter (see page 10). The efficiency of the drainage system should be checked when giving the pot or box a thorough watering. If the runaway between the crocks is in order and 'free', any excess of water will escape through the drainage holes. If the drainage system is faulty, the water will be held up and slow to disperse.

To check and correct a faulty drainage system once a window box is planted is difficult. It may be possible, with assistance, to lift up the box, and if the crocks are clogged, to scrape away with a sharp stick any soil material that is choking the crocks. Digging up the box in the middle of a flowering season should be the last resort, and only undertaken if the plants are dying. The gardener should make the best of things until the end of the season. Once he

50

knows that the drainage system is not functioning properly he must water with extra care, giving the plants short drinks that they can readily absorb.

Testing the drainage of a pot is a comparatively easy matter; it can be turned out and the crocks examined. Any fibre or soil holding up the runaway can be removed.

Watering. The number of plant casualties which result from the careless use of the watering-can is deplorable. Waterlogging is caused by the ignorant, who, without paying the slightest attention to the drainage system, turn the can upside down whenever it occurs to them. It is maltreatment a plant cannot stand; it can face feeling dry and thirsty for considerable periods, though it may show signs of strain, but with superabundance it dies in double-quick time. Water that is not easily evaporated is likely to cause decay. Always water gently and slowly and stop when the box or pot can absorb no more.

Rain water should be used whenever available. If the plants are in pots (see Chapter 8) on no account should water be allowed to remain in a saucer under the pot; this will surely kill. A layer of pebbles or peat in a tray under a window box or pot, that will absorb any excess of water, is beneficial.

When watering, do so liberally, except in winter; dribs and drabs bring roots to the surface and do more damage than good. Young plants, when first put into the box or pots, should be watered fairly generously, to firm their roots. After that, they need just enough to keep the soil mildy moist until they begin to grow away strongly. They then need plenty until, if perennials, they begin to go to rest, when the supply can be diminished.

Water should also be given before and after the application of any fertiliser, if not itself a liquid one.

Otherwise generalisations as to when to water are apt to be dangerous. Much depends on the temperature, the sun and the moisture of the atmosphere, the soil, the nature of the plant and the extent of its root structure, and lastly, and of primary importance, on the efficiency of the drainage system. If this is in good order, the gardener can water with a fairly easy conscience. Watering should be done in the morning as the temperature rises. Sun rays on wet leaves are liable to scorch them. A second watering may be needed when the sun goes down.

Although rain washes the foliage and gives plants a fresh look, if the foliage is excessive the moisture may not reach the roots, and the plants will still need watering.

The sheltered box under an overhanging roof, protected from the four drying winds, must also be watched to see it does not get thirsty.

WINDOW BOXES. During the winter months, provided that there is a normal rainfall, the box will need little watering. Once a week may suffice. Boxes vary, according to their position, as to the amount of rain they get. Plants prefer to be on the dry side during the hard and frosty weather. But bulbs must be watered carefully to see they do not go dry.

A box in a sunny position will dry out fast in the summer, and will need a good morning wetting, followed in the evening by a spray with a syringe or a second watering. Do not either flood the box or let it get bone dry; under-water rather than over-water, allowing the soil to dry out between each drink, and learn to gauge the happy medium.

POTS. Pots will not need much water during the winter months; perhaps once a week. It should be witheld during frost. Make sure that the water penetrates to the bottom of the pot. In summer, however, pots may require a thorough drenching morning and evening. They dry out much more quickly than window boxes. Some gardeners prefer to soak the pot for twenty minutes in a bucket of water in the morning and spray with a syringe in the evening.

The look and the feel of the foliage are useful guides; any limpness generally points to drought. Leaves should not be neglected and may be sponged over now and then, after they have been dusted. Plants catch the smuts more rapidly than ornaments do, and a flick with a feather duster is the remedy.

Gauging the moisture of a pot to discover if it needs watering is a comparatively easy matter. This can usually be done by simply lifting the pot to sense its weight. If it is very light, it needs water; if heavy-ish, not. A week or two of practice will train the gardener to judge. The other method, used by greenhouse gardeners, is to tap the pot with the knuckles. A hollow ring denotes that the earth is dry. A dull, sullen note indicates moisture.

Be mindful that the pot is a heat conductor, and that a powerful sun on a pot will evaporate all moisture in a surprisingly short time. Once soil bakes, it is difficult to soften it up and to make good the yawning cracks and breakaways from the pot's side. Water fairly gushes down through these openings and fissures, often by-passing the main roots.

Anti-drip trays and saucers must be emptied and not allowed to overflow (see page 5). There was a court case of a neighbour's drip driving a man to drink.

THE WINDOW BOX DECORATOR OR CONTRACTOR'S METHOD. There are several window box firms today who are decorators rather than gardeners and are merely concerned with prolonging the flower performance of a planting.

Their undertaking is to maintain the display in the box as long as possible and to see that the plants at no time dry out. What happens to the plants when they cease to flower does not concern them.

The decorator dispenses with drainage holes and lines the box with polythene so that the water cannot get away. This method requires clever judgment in watering by the maintenance staff: too much water would defeat the object and spell disaster.

Sun and shade. Most plants like the sun and do best when stationed in a window-box facing south, but there are a few, such as the primula family and others mentioned in the lists in Chapter 7, that thrive best in partial shade. The midday sun on a hot summer day is often too powerful for such plants. Here is a real problem; it is incredibly difficult to shelter an exposed window box adequately from the fierce rays. The gardener may attempt an umbrella arrangement as protection, but a light wind will play havoc with this. An envelope erected on a stick, although not decorative, provides certain shade for a single plant. Paper or material stretched out resting on stakes will protect a number of plants. Seedlings, the young and newly planted, must receive first attention.

If the gardener sees young plants wilting in the middle of the day, he must act quickly. A sheet of newspaper, though somewhat untidy, will suffice as a temporary shelter; tiffany sacking is good protection, light and easy to handle. Few of these improvisations are wholly satisfactory and none compete with the shade of a mossy bank in a wood.

Fertilisers. The busy time for fertilising is before the flowering season. Some plants suffer from exhaustion after flowering and may appreciate a mild dose of fertiliser, but this is the exception rather than the rule. Take care not to flog a plant to further effort with a chemical stimulant when by the law of nature it should be lying dormant, enjoying a well-deserved rest after flowering. Requirements during these inactive periods are practically nil: a low diet and the right to repose. For some unknown reason the beginner always has a tendency to over-fertilise. The meanest of men will be found to be generous with the fertiliser tin. No fertiliser should be necessary for a month after planting.

Farmyard manure, as long as it is well rotted, is unsurpassed, but it is hard to come by in towns; the sweepings from circus or tournament may be found to contain more empty ice-cream cartons than humus. In any case it takes a long time to rot down. It should be used sparingly later, otherwise there will be too much foliage and too few flowers. The other organic manures – fish meal, meat meal, dried blood, hoof-and-horn meal and bonemeal – are obtainable from the sundriesman with full instructions. I particularly recommend hoof-and-horn, which keeps well, is clean to handle but is slow in action. Dried blood is excellent for starting off plants in the spring. Bonemeal at sowing or planting time is excellent and does not burn roots; it acts slowly.

Artificial manures have three chief ingredients: nitrogen for foliage, an overdose of which will produce leaves at the expense of flowers (and for this reason window box gardeners should beware of dried blood); phosphorus is first rate for flowers and roots; potash for general health and resistance to disease. A general fertilizer usually consists of these three in the ratio of 1 : 2 : 1 and any recognised brand will serve for all ordinary purposes. Instructions for use are on the packet. Liquid fertilisers are particularly suitable for window boxes and pots. A mild solution should be mixed and kept stirred until used. Examples of these are Maxicrop, Liquinure, Fison's Liquid Green Solu-Feed, and Luxigro. Some window box nurserymen introduce a taste of Bio directly under a plant when planting, and I recommend Liquinure for seeds. In cities hydrated lime counteracts smoke pollution, while wood ash or soot, watered in, promotes healthy growth.

Foliar feeding should be given if a quick result is wanted.

If a plant seems content, leave it alone till just before flowering, when it will welcome a pick-me-up once or twice a week till flowering ends. Never feed a sick plant, one newly planted, or one that is resting after flowering. When anything is wrong, look for faulty drainage, bad aeration or tired soil before hurrying off to buy a fertilizer.

Pests and diseases. Cleanliness maintains health. Health gives resistance. When plants are attacked in spite of the gardener's care, he should consult a sundriesman immediately about a spray or dust to counteract the enemy. Derris, in liquid or powder form, is a good and safe general insecticide. Poisonous insecticides must be kept under lock and key.

'Damping off' is a sudden wilting of seedlings at soil level. A copper fungicide such as Cheshunt compound should be used.

Bud-dropping just before the flower-buds open should be treated not as a disease but as a sign of general ill health. It is usually caused by irregular watering – too little followed by too much.

The gardener should not grudge time taken in keeping his plants clean; cleanliness is as important to a plant as it is to a human being. Regular sponging of leaves, with warm water and, if necessary, a little soft soap, removes the grime which so quickly collects on a window-sill and its occupants. The arrival of insect or pest should be noted straight away and immediate action taken. Soft soap and water at an early stage will often do the trick.

Tidying. Trimming, or 'pinching' a plant into shape when the shoots are young, will save hard pruning later on. The symmetry of some plants is preserved by pinching out the tips of shoots while they are tender and soft; bushiness is assisted by snubbing the top shoot or leader. However, this is by no means a practice that is suitable for all plants. The beginner had better refrain until he has learnt something about the habits of each, otherwise he will be in danger of dismissing the next season's bloom.

Dead-heading is an important operation, particularly where annuals are concerned. Flower heads are better picked off too soon rather than too late. (See page 41.)

Window box weeding is not heavy work. Weeds should be destroyed soon after germination or at least before they seed, and perennial weeds with underground stems are more easily pulled up after watering.

Staking. Plants that are inclined to flop need what Shakespeare's gardener calls 'some supportance'. This requires a little knack. A plant bunched up like an obese woman uncomfortably corseted is by no means an unusual sight; or a window box with a whole scaffolding of sticks with each stalk held in a vice, and stakes towering above the flower heads.

The aim when tying a plant is not only to give it support but to improve its line. The stake should be inserted close to the stem without interfering with its roots. The shoots should be spread out and various slants and angles tried until a well-balanced effect is achieved. The outer shoots can be tied to their respective stakes first: each shoot will require a split cane or stake to itself. The supports should be slightly shorter than the shoots, reaching to the bottom of the flower spike.

Brushwood stakes are easy to handle and attract less notice than bamboo canes. Annuals can be grown through hazel twigs, which give effective and unobtrusive support.

Tying a plant is not unlike arranging a vase of flowers; the gardener should bear in mind that he is presenting a plant and blossom display and not advertising goods on behalf of a stake manufacturer. He should endeavour to hide the stakes behind the foliage.

The stems must be tied securely, but allowance should be made for growth and swelling. There must be a minimum of shackles; much depends on the height of the plant, but two ties to a one-foot plant should suffice. The bass or garden string should be looped round the stake, passed round the plant, and then returned to the stake, where the knot should be tied. The knot should be made against the stake and not next to the stem of the plant. The ties should be inspected throughout the growing season and loosened when necessary.

Pruning. This is a controversial subject, but of no great concern to the window box grower if he pinches and trims. The inexperienced gardener should concentrate on cutting out dead wood and encouraging new growth from the base of the plant. He should keep his secateurs sharp (a knife requires more skill and training) and use them rarely and with great discretion.

Division. This operation concerns perennials, and, as in pruning, there is a city and a country technique. In the country division is a regular autumnal event in the border, the perennials having encroached upon each other to their mutual detriment. But in the city window box where the plants do not grow rapidly, and resent being disturbed, it is often wise to leave well alone. The strong can be prevented from ousting the weak by snubbing the overpushing without embarking on any drastic change of place.

However, should division be decided upon, the operation should be less violent in the window box than in the border, and the spring rather than the autumn recommended as the best time for the shuffle round. When the plant is dug up the loose soil may be shaken away from the roots so that they can be thoroughly examined. It can then be cut into several parts with a sharp knife each part being supplied with an adequate root structure. The outside roots are young and superior to the old crown. and will produce the best flowers and following season. The plant can be torn or pulled apart rather than cut asunder; some plants such as the double daisy or the primrose lend themselves more readily to this method than to the knife.

The aster, or michaelmas daisy, fibrous-rooted and easily divided, is recommended to the novice for his first experiment.

Cuttings and layering. Cuttings and layering are often mentioned in this book as the best means of propagation. Unfortunately, there was not room for a chapter on this subject. The novice should consult an expert whenever possible.

Removal. Bulbs, once they have flowered, are invariably in the way. Those who can afford to buy afresh for the following season should dig them up and send them off to a friend in the country. They seldom give a good performance their second year and if left will delay the summer bedding planting.

Gardeners who wish to make their bulbs serve a second year are often in a predicament. There is seldom a place in a flat or town house where the bulbs can be suitably stored and given the air, light and an occasional watering they need.

It is necessary for the bulbs to remain covered with soil and undisturbed until the foliage dies back naturally. This will take some months, as soon as the leaves die down the bulbs may be lifted (some time after June).

Annuals, having completed their lives, can only be thrown away. They seldom flower more than 10–12 weeks.

Perennials should be cut back in late autumn and grown on. The half-hardy, such as fuchsia and the geranium, must be brought indoors before the frost. They can be potted or placed in shallow boxes or trays. Fuchsia (see page 95). Geranium (see page 98).

10   The Window Rock Garden

There was some time ago an attractive rock garden window box in Kensington. There were peaks, a pool of water and a winding path, but a minimum of bridges and pagodas. The rocks, deeply embedded in the soil, were of nice old brick. One or two of them jutted out beyond the edge of the box; the designer had managed to give the slopes a natural appearance, and the gardener had covered them with different shaded pinks, saxifrages, and sedums.

Far more important than the landscape were the many comfortable crevices, well packed with fibrous soil, which had been put at the disposal of the alpines. These neat growers only require a crack or fissure to satisfy them, and here the architect had provided a record number of corners in a limited space. The gardener told me that he had sprinkled the soil with coarse sand throughout the winter, and had remade the top soil twice during the year. As a result the box was in flower from February to October; he was proud of having worked over-time.

Building the garden. The rocks and their arrangements are the first consideration. There are a number of materials available, and in choosing them appearance and porosity are important factors. The more porous the material the more congenial will it be to the alpines. Coal clinkers, however, should not be included.

Suitable shapes have to be picked out for the alpine summits and mountain slopes.

Laying the stones on the top of the soil is useless; they have to be firmly planted so that they cannot be disturbed by the rain or the watering-can, or jolted out of place by the gardener's trowel. They must be solidly embedded, and well over half of their surface buried and the soil rammed tightly against the rocks. In the course of time the surface soil is washed away by watering and the stones become exposed; the gardener is advised to replenish with fresh soil otherwise a landslide is inevitable.

The design should allow for plenty of planting space and a host of snug corners; but the rocks should be placed at such an angle that the plants get the rain and the benefit of the watering-can without getting too much of either The rocky slopes should be gentle enough to allow for a quiet flow of water and for this the right incline has to be discovered; the stones must slope back at an easy angle. Be sure that the moisture can reach the plant roots and that there is an escape for any overflow. Alpines fade away at any suspicion of sourness or damp. They suffer from mountain nostalgia and miss their rest beneath the snow.

The common fault of the novice is to be too generous with his rocks. Whatever their number the soil cannot be too firmly tucked around them, thus avoiding air pockets and loose root runs.

Mountain peaks and ranges may be kept clean by wiping them over occasionally with soap and water, and if necessary a little Vim.

Soil. Soil for mountain plants can be bought from a good nurseryman, and is usually composed as follows:

3 parts sterilised light loam;
1 part coarse sand;
1 part peat.

The following home-made compost should suit all but the most fastidious:

3 parts loam;
1 part coarse sand;
1 part peat or leaf-mould;
a sprinkling of mortar rubble, charcoal, chips, and seashell.

Getting the plants. If the gardener has the opportunity of visiting an alpine specialist at a nursery, discussing the matter with the expert and coming away with a pot in hand, it is the ideal way of doing things. The pot plant is infinitely preferable to one brought with its roots loose and dangling.

Another good way of buying these small plants is at flower shows, where on the last day many of the exhibits, beautifully grown plants little the worse for wear, are often for sale at a moderate price. It is helpful to mark a catalogue at the Chelsea Show or Southport or the Royal Horticultural Society's shows as it can then be referred to later when making purchases. The enthusiast should join the Alpine Garden Society[1] or the Scottish Rock Garden Club.[2]

Planting. The best time for planting alpines is the spring or autumn. Throughout this book I stress my preference for spring planting for London.

[1] 296 Vauxhall Bridge Rd, London, S.W.1.
[2] Boonslie, Dirleton, East Lothian.

There are exceptions among early spring flowers such as the primulas, which are best transplanted after flowering.

It is hoped that the advantage of buying pot plants has also been made clear; it enables the gardener to plant at any time of the year (other than the height of summer) without acute disturbance to roots.

It is important when dealing with mountain plants to plant them firmly. Vandals like myself, who have ravaged the Swiss mountains or the slopes of the Haute Savoie, know how close and tight to the earth the alpines cling. They strongly resent being dug up and when they give in because they must they present themselves in rootless tufts or torn and ugly pieces.

The rocks should be used skilfully to show off the plants, and the crevice-lovers must be found suitable places where they can be tightly yet comfortably wedged in. A few stone chips placed round the collars of a plant will help to keep it snug and dry.

Depressions in the stones and bricks can be filled with soil and then planted with sedums or silver-webbed *Sempervivums* (house leeks). These manage with a minimum of soil so long as a suggestion of nourishment and just sufficient moisture are provided.

In selecting and placing the alpines there should be a fair balance between spring and summer flowers so that the box is never dull.

Care and welfare. The rockery-box needs more than occasional attention; and no one should attempt it unless he is prepared to take a lot of trouble. Debris and dead stalks should be regularly removed and a taste of powdered limestone given to those who like it. Much can be done to help the plants with the aid of a blunt knife and kitchen fork by keeping the soil well aerated, and the whole landscape sweet and clean. It is wiser to remove any sour top soil rather than to attempt to neutralise it with fertiliser; it should be replaced by fibrous loam with a generous grit content. As the soil is washed away by rain and watering, it must be replaced and the roots re-covered before the plant has an opportunity of withering. The watering-can must be used sparingly until the plants are established.

It will be found that some of the tufts and stone-loving species have a habit of developing bare patches (usually in the centre of the plant): these bald places must be top-dressed (mulched) with sandy leaf-mould to encourage fresh growth. If the trouble persists the plant should be divided up in the spring.

In many instances old plants have to be replaced by young ones. Propagation is affected by cutting or division. Many of the alpines can be readily pulled apart in the spring.

It is a triumph to keep the alpines going in a big city throughout the winter;

59

rarities are amusing, but as a rule temperamental and difficult. Rain and fog are the main winter troubles, and a sheet of glass rested on small stakes provides certain protection for any particular plant. This arrangement works wonders.

Expert selections

Two rockery experts have been kind enough to pick out plants that they consider suitable for this work. Note how they have avoided rampageous plants, such as *Saponaria ocymoides* and *Polygonum vacciniifolium*. Be careful about this if you make you own choices.

Mr F. A. Robinson's twenty-four:

Pimelea coarctata. New Zealand Daphne, White. 3 in.
Mentha requienii. Creeping mint, mauve. ¼ in.
Lewisia hybrid. Pink and apricot, 2–3 in.
Jasminum parkeri. Yellow miniature, 6 in.
Fuchsia 'Tom Thumb'. Hardy dwarf, 9 in.
Salix arbuscula. Dwarf willow, yellow catkins. 6 in.
Sedum lidakense. Pink and red heads. 4 in.
Spiraea bullata. Small crimson shrub. 9 in.
Thymus minus. Small creeping thyme, pink. ¼ in.
Erodium reichardii 'Roseum'. Pink Heron's Bill. 2–3 in.
Miniature Rose. Various colours, 6–9 in.
Gentiana septemfida. Deep blue trumpets. 6 in.
Dianthus 'Little Jock'. Double pink, deep centre. 4 in.
Sisyrinchium 'Ball's Mauve'. Iris-like. 4 in.
Saxifraga 'Peter Pan' Moss, deep red. 3–4 in.
Allium marei. Dainty pink mountain garlic. 4 in.
Anacyclus depressus. Mount Atlas Daisy, white, scarlet reverse, 2–3 in.
Armeria 'Beechwood'. Dwarf pink thrift. 4 in.
Cytisus decumbens. Yellow creeping broom. 2–3 in.
Campanula hallii. Dangling white bells. 3 in.
Cyananthus microphyllus. Powder blue flowers. 1 in.
Frankenia thymaefolia. Tiny pink creeper. 1 in.
Hebe pinguifolia 'Pagei'. Glaucous blue shrub, white flowers. 6 in.
Helianthemum alpestre. Yellow creeping shrublet. 3 in.

Mr Will Ingwersen names twelve plants chosen to give a long flowering season and attractive foliage when the box is not in bloom.

Phlox 'Temiscaming'. Crimson.
Potentilla tonguei. Terracotta with five crimson spots.
Antennaria 'Nyewood variety'. Silvery foliage and pink flowers.
Campanula carpatica. Rich blue.
Dianthus deltoides. Red flowers.
Erigeron mucronatus. Pink and white daisy flowers over a very long period.
Erinus 'Dr Hanele'. Rich red.
Genista pilosa procumbens. A creeping broom with golden-yellow flowers.
Phlox douglasii rosea. Soft pink.
Sedum spathulifolium purpureum. Purple leaves and rich yellow flowers.
Saxifraga 'Boston Spa'. Green cushions and primrose coloured flowers.
Campanula 'E. H. Frost'. Soft pale blue.

Bulbs

Anemone blanda. Blue. 4 in. March–April.
A. b. rosea. Pink; tuberous-rooted perennial. Plant in October. 4 in. March–April.
Crocus balansae. Orange and buff. 2 in.; February–March
C. sativus. Purple. 2 in.; October–November.
C. tomasinianus. Lavender blue. 4 in.; February–March.
Cyclamen coum. Rose, magenta. 3 in.; January–March.
C. album. White. 3 in.; January–March.
C. europaeum. Crimson. 4 in.; July–August.

Plant cyclamen corms during their resting period. June to August for autumn-flowering and July to November for spring-flowering varieties. Shade is essential during summer months. The best results are to be had from young corms.

Narcissus bulbocodium conspicuus. Golden-yellow. 5 in.; March–April.
N. triandrus albus (Angel's Tears). Cream-white. 4 in.; March–April.
N. minimus. Golden. 2 in.; March–April (minute).
N. cyclamineus. Yellow; requires plenty of moisture. Some gardeners will have seen this bulb naturalized and in great beauty. 4 in.; March–April.
Iris histrioides major. Royal blue and gold. 4 in.; February–March.
I. reticulata. Violet; sweet-scented. 6 in.; February–March.

Unless otherwise stated, the bulbs may be planted in the autumn. Other bulbs, most of them suitable for the rockery, are to be found in the bulb chapter. Small bulbs are ideal, among them, the winter-flowering crocus, the autumn crocus, chionodoxa, aconite, fritillaria, snowdrop, grape hyacinth, and the small scillas. These look charming among the rosettes and cobwebs of the sempervivums.

Dwarf shrubs

Dwarfs for the rockery should be chosen for their slow growth and hardiness. If evergreens are required, junipers will provide neat columns that break the line. (See Winter box, pages 70–3) I add only:

Azalea rosiflora (*Rhododendron roseum*). Pink, double. Requires a little shelter and is not for the colder counties. 9–12 in.; June.

11   Salads in the Window

The salad box is entertaining rather than profitable, and outdoor tomatoes are rewarding only in a good summer. The early lettuce always give it a pleasant, cool look.

The tomato. The tomato is a tender annual, a native of tropical South America and for many years looked upon as a poisonous fruit. It is a sun-loving and accommodating plant, and 'Money Maker' is a splendid variety with well-set trusses of medium-sized fruit of average flavour. I used to recommend Market King, a heavy cropper with round medium-sized fruit, but now feel that 'Sunrise' and 'Harbinger' are better varieties for the box, being less vigorous and in many ways superior. 'Dwarf Gem' (spaced 15 in. apart) is an excellent window-box subject. The new 'Outdoor Girl' should be fine.

Buying. The gardener must look out for strong young seedlings, bushy plants of about 10 in. in height, that have been well grown and carefully hardened off, which he can transplant into his box towards the end of May or the beginning of June. The darkish green short-jointed plantlets are the ones to go for, and much will depend upon a wise selection. Pot-grown seedlings are preferable, as they do not suffer any acute disturbance from the move.

When buying, allow approximately 12 in. space for each plant; three plants are often more comfortable in the window box than four.

The gardener who raises his own seedlings will sow in the middle of April for fruiting in July.

Culture. Any ordinary good soil capable of retaining moisture will suit the tomato. It is as well to avoid rich fresh manure at this early stage, or the plant is likely to put all its energy into rank growth rather than into flower and fruit. Two parts decayed turfy loam and one part decomposed manure is the compost usually recommended; a sprinkling of bonemeal can be usefully added to the compost to give it a more lasting balance. The box should be filled only two-thirds full of soil, leaving plenty of room for top-dressing.

The seedlings require firm planting about 12 in. apart, and will need protection from the sun until they are rooted.

When new growth begins, side shoots should be rubbed out, with finger and thumb, so that the plant's entire strength may go into the leader. The stem should be tied to a 4 ft stake and not permitted to grow beyond this.

During the flowering period the plants require to be tapped at midday with a stick; this fertilises the bloom.

Once the fruit has set, feeding should begin in earnest, tired soil may be scraped away and a top dressing of rich loam compost with a basis of decayed manure should be applied. If artificial manure is to be used, a weekly dose of a tablespoonful of superphosphate and half a tablespoonful of sulphate of potash to a box holding about a bushel of soil makes an excellent stimulant; if watered in with soot water, so much the better. Alternatively, use a proprietary tomato fertiliser.

Water sparingly until the first fruit has set, then freely and regularly. Capricious watering is liable to cause the fruit to crack. As it matures, take care that the leaves do not obstruct the sun's rays; if they are in the way they can be pushed aside. Tomatoes that have failed to ripen by September may be picked off and placed in the sun to colour.

The trouble with the tomato is that it takes up too much of the window, the air, and light for the fresh-air fiend.

Lettuce. The lettuce was introduced in 1562. There are two types: the cabbage and the cos. The cabbage lettuce is the better for the window-box, being more compact. The cos is a greedy feeder with deep roots, and takes up a great deal of room.

Varieties of the cabbage lettuce that can be recommended are: 'Arctic King', crisp and well formed; 'Webb's Wonderful' is large, early, a good colour and a great favourite, but I prefer 'Unrivalled', a solid, compact early maturing type or 'Tom Thumb', the dwarf of the family.

'Paris White' is my pick of the cos varieties; it does not run to seed as readily as some.

Miller Gault recommends 'Little Gem', sometimes known as 'Sugar Cos'.

'Winter Density' is an intermediate variety between the cabbage and cos; it is crisp and has a good solid heart.

Culture. The lettuce likes a rich loamy soil, and plenty of water during the dry months. Seedlings are easy to come by from April onwards, and are stronger if grown in the country. They should be planted 10 in. apart, watered freely and dosed with a nitrate fertiliser when the plants show growth. Two such doses in a lifetime, with a fortnight in between, is all the plant will need.

The gardener who grows his own seedlings has the advantage of sowing at intervals and so growing a succession of crops; he can sow from March to the end of July. A lettuce will mature within eleven weeks.

Mustard and cress. Mustard, a biennial, and cress, an annual, can be bought ready mixed; but epicures prefer to buy separately as the mustard germinates a little faster than the cress, taking only ten days to reach the cutting stage, while cress takes a fortnight. Salad-growing gardeners sow a small amount of these seeds from March to late September; they usually sow two successive crops on the same soil.

'Finest White' is an excellent mustard variety for flavouring salad; mixed with either plain-leaved or curled cress. Seed can be bought by the ounce or pint.

Culture. Mustard and cress will grow almost anywhere, but always seem to do best in shallow boxes. The first sowing can be made towards the end of March.

The cress should be sown from two to four days before the mustard, and the seeds scattered evenly on the surface of lightly sieved soil; they require no covering but should be pressed down with a board clamp, after which they may be watered.

The crop is ready for cutting when an inch high.

Spring onions. 'White Lisbon' is a well-flavoured onion for salads.

Seeds should be sown a quarter of an inch deep, in lines during early April. Pulling can begin as soon as the gardener thinks fit.

Radishes. Radishes were among the first vegetables ever cultivated; they are a hardy annual, and usually a catch crop grown in the shadow of the lettuce. French Breakfast is a desirable variety, bright scarlet with a white tip. Early Red and Early White seed may be bought from any reputable seedsman.

Pull when young and tender.

Culture. The radish enjoys a light rich soil and a sunny position in the early spring and late autumn. The seed should be surface sown, and only lightly covered with sieved soil; afterwards it should be made firm with a board clamp.

As soon as the seedlings are large enough to handle (about 1 in. high) they should be drastically thinned out.

Successional sowing may be begun in February and should end in October. If sown in spring, the seed will germinate within a week. A tonic of superhosphate will help production.

Parsley and Chives. An edging of parsley will give tone to the planting and the chives an extra flavour.

Beets. Beet fans may care to add a round beet, such as 'Boltardy', to their crop.

12   A Window Herb Garden

From the middle of the seventeenth century the gardener had his attention diverted from the herb garden to a new vogue – the flower bed. But today herbs are back in fashion, thanks to the amateur cooks with sensitive palates, and a willingness to adventure. There are cooks who use a pelargonium leaf – the oak-leaf *Pelargonium capitatum* – to give a subtler flavour to a plain cake.

Those who are appreciative of good food will know the value of home-grown herbs. They are capable of making many dull foods exciting.

There are gardeners who throw their whole window box open to herbs; others keep a special corner of the box for them or do their growing in separate pots. The aromatic scent of thyme blowing into the room is the reward for our trouble.

Culture. Good ordinary soil with compost added and kept well aerated, will suffice; regular and generous watering throughout the dry season is essential. Those that are not annuals should be divided at least every three years; they can be treated as ordinary herbaceous perennials. City growers are advised to buy young plants or seedlings from the nurseryman in the spring.

Harvesting. Herbs should be gathered for drying before they come into flower, when their flavour is most pronounced. There are exceptions to this rule: tarragon, for instance, has to be picked in August.

I recommend the gathering of small bunches at different times, rather than just the one harvest. Shoots should be picked in the morning before the sun is on the plants, and loosely tied together so that the air can get at the leaves. They must be dry at the time of gathering.

Herbs are best spread out on trays of hessian or perforated zinc. On no account should they be roasted in the sun.

It is a proud gardener who can gather half a dozen different herbs from his window box; tying them up in muslin, he may drop them, a 'broth posie', into a simmering stew.

Balm. The *Melissa*, or common balm, is a hardy perennial with strong aromatic foliage; there is also an attractive variegated variety; 2 to 3 ft. The leaves are used for flavouring soups, stews, salad or a red wine cup. Stems can be gathered when the flowers are open and the leaves dried for winter use. A rather tall plant for the box.

Balm likes good soil and plenty of moisture. Plant October or March. Once the flowering season is over, the plant should be cut down to the ground: propagation by division of roots in October or March.

Bergamot. A hardy perennial and one of the most decorative herbs with red, pink or purple flowers. Height, 1 ft. The leaves and flowers are edible for salads, tea, and mixed with cress as a sandwich filling. It is another rather tall plant that should be kept cut back.

Moist loam soil and partial shade suit bergamot. Plant in March or April: propagation by division in autumn or spring.

Borage. A hardy annual, height, 12 to 18 in. The leaves are excellent for flavouring claret, 'Pimm's No. 1', and other cups. The very young foliage can be used for salad. Borage does well on ordinary fare. Annuals may be bought each spring as seedlings or can be grown from seed.

Chervil. An annual with cut leaves and sprays of small white flowers. 1 ft. The leaves are used for flavouring for soups, stews, and salads.

Seeds may be sown either in March (or October under glass).

Chives. A bulbous-rooted hardy perennial successful even in towns. It is a low and tidy-growing member of the onion family but more delicate in taste. The giant chive of similar flavour and grass-green appearance is worth growing; it comes into season after the ordinary chive is over, and is useful edging for the front of the box. The foliage has a wonderful onion flavouring; indispensable for omelettes, salads, and seasoning.

Ordinary soil will do. Planting should take place in March: propagation by division every three years.

Dandelion. A hardy perennial; somewhat out of fashion. Young leaves are a pleasant addition to a spring salad. Dandelion tea was once considered wholesome for those suffering from liver complaints.

Give the dandelion ordinary soil, free from manure, and a sunny position. Propagation by seed sown in April.

Fennel. A hardy perennial herb. Tall growing; about 2–3 ft. The leaves are famous for fish sauces, salads, and garnishing. Some cooks use fennel seed for flavouring soup.

Plant in March or April in ordinary soil and a sunny position: propagation by seed sown in April. Flowers should be removed as they form unless seed is required.

Marjoram. French marjoram, a perennial, is a cook's favourite; 2 ft. The leaves are useful for flavouring soups.

Marjoram likes ordinary good soil and a sunny position. Plant in March; top dress each spring: propagation by division in the autumn.

Mint. A hardy perennial highly valued in the kitchen. The variety most usually grown is spearmint. Height, about 2 ft, but it should be cut before it reaches this height. The plant varies in quality, and it is important to grow a well-flavoured variety. Freshly chopped mint from the window-box is delicious and compares favourably with that bought at the shop. Spearmint – *Mentha spicata* – is usually the basis of ordinary mint sauce. Epicures prefer apple mint (*M. rotundifolia*), but this grows to some 4 ft and is too rampant and big for the window box. *M. longifolia* and *M. sylvestris* (horsemint) are ready for picking before spearmint; they are useful for sauce early in the season, if slightly inferior in flavour. The leaves are used for sauce, seasoning (sage and onion stuffing), and flavouring.

The family enjoys a rich moist soil and a sunny position or partial shade. Plant in the spring; water freely throughout the summer. The stems should be cut down in September and soil top-dressed with rich compost: propagation by division in autumn or spring or by cutting during the early summer.

Parsley. A hardy biennial; appetising and a gay and low-growing edging for the box. 'Triple Curled', 8 to 12 in., and 'Green Gem', 5 in., are valuable varieties.

Parsley needs rich soil, well drained: plant in the spring. Likes partial shade but objects to damp and too much soot. When leaves coarsen they should be cut back to induce young growth. Propagation: by seed, best sown for succession from February to late summer. The seedlings are sometimes slow in appearing; they should be drastically thinned out when an inch high. The novice seldom allows the seedlings enough room to develop. Failure with parsley is often due to lack of lime, which it appreciates.

Sage. A hardy perennial. The Broad-leaf, non-flowering sage is the best culinary variety. It can be kept bushy and nicely shaped by pinching back young shoots. Height, about 2 ft. The leaves are useful as flavouring for soup, seasoning, and tea.

Sage likes the sun but will tolerate partial shade and ordinary soil. Plant in March. Old plants deteriorate, and spring cuttings (with a heel when possible) should be taken each year. Seeds sown in April or May germinate readily.

Sorrel. A perennial. Height, about 2 ft. The large-leafed French 'Oseille de Belville' is best for kitchen use. This is a large plant for the window box and may be dropped from the list or confined to a pot. Sorrel leaves are used for flavouring soup or salad.

Plant in March in ordinary soil and a sunny position. Water freely throughout the summer. Flower stems should be removed as soon as they appear, and leaves gathered frequently: propagation by division in the spring, or by seed in March.

Tarragon. A perennial. 2 ft. A good-looking, tall plant requiring plenty of room. The French variety is recommended. The leaves can be used for salad dressing, vinegar, and for flavouring egg dishes. Leaves picked in August or September can be dried off for winter use.

Plant in October or March in ordinary dry soil in a sunny position: propagation by division in the spring or by cuttings (with a heel to them when possible) taken in August or September.

Thyme. A hardy perennial. Common thyme, the lemon-scented, and the silver and golden variegated forms are all about 6–9 in. high. No *bouquet garni* is complete without thyme. Bushy in habit, it makes an excellent edging for the box. Young shoots should be gathered during the flowering season and kept for winter use.

Thyme likes rich soil and a warm sunny position. Plant in March or April and water freely through the summer. Some gardeners confine thyme to a pot within the box to keep it under control and to be able to water it more freely. Most varieties will divide in the spring, but the gold and silver thymes are best increased by cuttings grown in the cool frames of country friends.

Suggestions for a six-herb box.

French marjoram
Lemon thyme
Mint
Parsley
Rosemary
Sage

Mint and thyme are trespassers and will have to be kept in their place: trimmings can be used for winter drying.

13   The Winter Box

This box has grown in popularity and gardeners are no longer satisfied with a long dead season and an empty box. It is pleasant to have something green to look at throughout the winter; this is easily managed by the gardener in possession of a duplicate box. Those who are fortunate in this can have a real winter box planted with evergreens that are permanent residents. Town gardeners have seldom more than one box and are concerned with converting their summer or autumn display into a winter one.

The change-over. The time for the change-over has to be carefully chosen. Evergreens should be in their place by October if they are to establish and fortify themselves before winter conditions set in. This often means sacrificing late-flowering plants that are still giving a good performance, in order to make room for the shrubs. If you keep your autumn box too long you may lose the pick of the evergreens at the nursery. Demand for these plants starts in the second half of September and reaches a crescendo in October.

It is a problem to know what to do with the summer plants such as the fuchsias and geraniums; some dry, well-ventilated spot indoors must be found for them, unless accommodating country friends are prepared to give them a home under glass until they are wanted again. They should be potted up or boxed and put discretely out of sight.

How to buy. The dwarf conifers and small evergreens have become deservedly popular not only for window boxes but for rockeries and miniature gardens. Nurserymen specialise in these shrubs and there is a wide choice available in grey, olive, yellow-green and silver-blue among the spruce firs and cypresses. Unlike flowering plants, they may be viewed the whole year round, and the best way is for the gardener to pay a visit to the nursery.

The shrub and evergreen list is a long one, in which the dwarf conifers take first place. These miniature shrubs vary tremendously in shape and manner of growth. Unlike the dwarfs from Japan, they are not artificially stunted but are by nature dwarf in habit. They grow slowly and transplant well, usually being pot-grown. As to shape, there are columns, bushes, pyramids, cones and low-growing or prostrate forms. If the dwarf character of the conifer is to be retained, they are best raised from cuttings rather than grafted. A graft can be detected by examining the main stem at ground level, where there will be a slight swelling.

Plants in the window box are more exposed than those in the shrubbery and must be tough.

Culture. Provided the evergreen is given a good ordinary compost and not allowed to get dry, it is by no means exacting.

If the root ball is found to be parched, it should be well soaked before planting. Wiry outside roots may be cut back in moderation to induce fresh growth and the fibrous roots gently spread out, and fine soil introduced among them. It is essential to plant firmly, after which a thorough watering can be given.

Evergreens, and conifers in particular, should never be allowed to become dry at the roots. If rain is lacking, they need copious watering during the warm months, especially during the late spring winds.

In the case of a grafted plant, any sucker must be cut back from wherever it rises; this is usually below ground level.

The soil must at all times be kept well broken up and open with as little root disturbance as possible.

The dwarf evergreens in a duplicate window box, that are permanents forming a background for spring bulbs, or those that stay on in the box throughout the year featuring with the bedders in the summer, should last two or three years if sponged or washed and regularly cared for. But unfortunately these small shrubs are often sadly neglected; one comes across numbers of them in London's streets choked with sooty deposit, crying aloud for a good wash and a fresh start.

The life of an evergreen that is put in during October and removed in May and moved back again in the autumn is too restless to be long; two years would be a fair average.

Bulbs placed among the evergreens add to the attractiveness of the box in spring. Narcissi look extraordinarily well with the dark shrubs; they can be planted and removed with the shrubs.

The change back. The shrubs and possibly bulbs should be out of the box by the third week in May to make room for the bedders. Once more, if it is possible to arrange with country friends to 'heel' the shrubs into the ground in some border (not in the full sun) until the autumn, so much the better. If not, they should be potted and carefully watered and well looked after during the summer. They can then be put in the well-ventilated spot where the fuchsias and the geraniums spent the winter.

The duplicate box. The duplicate box enables the plants to settle down and make a root run. Top dressed, and placed in partial shade somewhere in the country from May until October or November, it should indeed look its best when the time comes to bring it to the city.

The gardener will also feel justified in buying the rather more expensive and distinctive dwarfs, hoping that their life will be a reasonably long one.

The second box makes allowance for the early autumn planting of bulbs, and when they have flowered gives the leaves time to die back in peace. It is a luxury.

The experts choose

The heights of the dwarfs vary from 6 to 12 in.; according to their breeding, with a diameter of approximately similar measurement.

Mr H. G. Hillier, the well-known shrub expert of Hillier and Sons, Winchester, has kindly recommended suitable plants for the winter box.

Berberis panlanensis. A neat, compact and charming evergreen.
Cotoneaster microphyllus thymifolius. Small-leafed form. A good rock plant.
Euonymus fortunei 'Silver Queen'. Bright silver variegation.
Hypericum moseranum. A low ground cover shrub.
H. m. 'Tricolor'. Leaves prettily variegated white, pink and green.
Ilex cornuta. A low-growing Chinese species. Red berries on rare occasions.
Ilex crenata. Japanese holly. Small purple-black berries.
Jasminum nudiflorum. Yellow winter-flowering jasmine.
Mahonia aquifolium. The common species for sun or shade. Rich yellow flowers, blue-black berries.
Olearia mollis. Silver-grey foliage, musk scented.
Pernettya mucronata. White, lilac, red and purple berries.
Rhododendron impeditum. An excellent rock-garden shrub of low spreading habit. Small, cobalt violet flowers.
Sarcococca confusa. Elliptic leaves, white fragrant flowers and black fruit.
Senecio greyi. Silver-grey foliage, golden-yellow daisy flowers.
Skimmia japonica. Japanese bush, dome-shaped. Scarlet berries on female plant.

Mr L. R. Russell of Richmond Nurseries, London Road, Windlesham, Surrey, gives the following as his choices for the winter box.

Bergenia cordifolia and *B. cordifolia purpurea*. Glistening, leathery, purple leaves;

best collected from nursery personally, to ensure undamaged plants. Pink flowers in April. 9 in.

Buxus sempervirens. The well-known and reliable box. Small clipped pyramind plants recommended. 2 ft.

Elaeagnus pungens 'Maculata'. A handsome variegated, compact evergreen, the leaves splashed with gold. 18 in.

Fatsia japonica (syn. *Aralia sieboldii*). An evergreen for the larger box, with bold, glossy, light-green, palmate foliage of good form. 18 in.

Hedera helix 'Glacier' and *Hedera helix* 'Sheen Silver'. Two good small-leaved variegated ivies for front-row planting and trailing.

Ilex aquifolium pyramidalis. An upright green holly which is self-fertile, and can be bought loaded with berry in late October. Suitable for the larger box. 18 in.

Pernettya mucronata Davis's hybrids. Large pink and red berries. Best purchased personally from the nursery to make sure of berried plants. 1 ft. Must have acid, peaty soil.

Ruta graveolens 'Jackman's Blue'. A selected form of the culinary rue with blue-green foliage. Although not a true evergreen, its foliage holds on well into mid-winter. 9–12 in.

Skimmia japonica foremanii. Ideal evergreen with tough, orange-red berries which last all through the winter. Must be purchased with berries intact. 1 ft.

Hebe darwiniana. Bright grey foliage and compact habit. 1 ft.

Hebe sub-alpina. Pleasing apple-green foliage, very tough with pin-cushion habit. 1 ft.

I cannot resist adding my favourite miniature shrubs to the lists given – *Juniperus communis* 'Compressa', an attractive alpine conifer, closely columnar in habit; a real charmer, variegated *Hebe* with bronze leaves; *Chamaecyparis lawsoniana*, 'Elwood's Gold' (a fine form) and the *Solanum* (the cherry plant) that is likely to lose its foliage but hangs on to its bright orange-red berries. Perhaps I should mention the variegated *Aucuba*, a tough that will take a lot of bad treatment.

There is a far wider choice of shrubs and evergreens than there used to be and the gardener, when possible, should visit a nursery and choose the plants himself.

14   Colour Schemes and Fancy Boxes

In this chapter I shall deal with the permanent window box and with boxes for separate seasons and special purposes.

The permanent box

This is the townsman's window box; the gardener concerned lives in the city all but a week or two of the year, and aims at always having something in flower. Many of these gardeners will be unable to afford a clean sweep with each season and will have a number of permanent residents in their window boxes, some of which no doubt will be tall and leggy, but nevertheless capable of giving a creditable flower performance. The permanent-box gardener fills his box as occasion offers; a tidy-up in spring and a thorough renovation in the autumn is the normal programme. It is a box that must have care and attention when out of flower.

If there are two window boxes on the same level a certain uniformity of arrangement is more successful than planting the boxes with different flowers.

Some of the following plants, if not already of the party, might usefully be added to it when the autumn overhaul takes place.

IF MORE WHITE IS NEEDED

Anaphalis triplinervis. Silver foliage, snow-white flowers. 12 in. July–August.
Arabis albida. Single, double, and variegated; inclined to sprawl. Long flowering season. 4–8 in. June–August.
Aster (Michaelmas Daisy). Dwarf variety, 'Snow Cushion'; 8 in.; September–October.
Bellis perennis. Double daisy; 3–5 in.; April–July. See page 92.

Campanula. See page 93.
Dianthus. Pinks and carnations. See page 95.
Geranium. See page 97.
Iberis sempervirens (perennial candytuft). 1–2 ft. May.
Lily of the Valley.
Saxifrages. See page 102.

FOR MORE BLUES, PURPLES, AND MAUVES

Aster (Michaelmas Daisy). Dwarf varieties:

  'Autumn Princess'. Lavender-blue; 14 in.
  'Lilac Time'. 9 in.
  'Lady in Blue'. 12 in.
  'Queen of Sheba'. Pale pink suffused lilac; 10 in.

Aubrieta. See page 91.
Campanula. See page 93.
Gentian. For experienced gardeners only.
Iris. See pages 24–5.
Lavender, dwarf varieties, such as 'Hidcote'.
Primula. See page 100.
Viola odorata. Sweet-scented violet. Variety 'Princess of Wales'. Decayed leaves
  must be picked off. 6 in.; April–May.

FOR MORE PINKS AND REDS

  Miss Wendy Carlile of Lodden Nurseries, Carlile's Corner, Twyford, Berks,
gives the following suggestions.

Dwarf Michaelmas Daisies: 'Pink Lace', 4 in.; 'Jenny', red, 12 in.; 'Nancy',
  pale pink, 9 in.; 'Rosebud', the best pink dwarf, 12–15 in. and 'Terry's
  Pride', cerise, 12 in.

  This dwarf group of hybrids is ideal for the window box through September
and October.

Begonias. See page 92.
Bellis perennis. See page 92.
Pinks and carnations. See page 95.
Fuchsia. See pages 95–7.
Geranium. See pages 97–8.
Sedum spectabile. Stonecrop. Variety 'Brilliant'. Rose pink. Large flat heads that
  attract the butterflies. 15 in. August–October.

Chrysanthemum koreanum. Small-flowered Koreans (best wintered under glass) can be grown in sheltered positions (see page 94). August–October.

Gazania. A number of tangerine and orange hybrids. For a sunny position; rarely survives a city winter. 6–12 in. June–October.

Iris. See pages 24–5.

Polyanthus and Primrose. See pages 100–1 (Primulas).

Viola. See page 103.

FOR MORE GREEN

Hosta (Plantain Lily). Deep green, blue-green, or white-edged, with pale lilac flowers in August. The leaves are noble, the flowers somewhat insignificant. Excellent for shady moist positions. 18–24 in.

Lonicera nitida and its gold form are effective and not so greedy as privet.

Privet. The green or golden privet. 12–18 in. I must confess that since childhood I have thoroughly disliked this plant and its greedy ways. But recently a professional window box gardener took me to see what use she had made of it in a series of window boxes. I was amazed and converted straight away. Here were small, well-groomed, yellow hedges standing at the back of various bright-coloured flower compositions; a delightful background for petunias, geraniums or lobelia. In another box it was showing off deep purple violas. This was a new departure in arrangement, attractive and cheap. I was told and can well believe that the gay yellow hedge looked charming behind forget-me-nots in the spring. I have much pleasure in recommending the golden privet.

Saxifraga. See page 102.

Sedum telephium. See page 102. Stonecrop. 12 in. Also other species and varieties.

So much for colour. If there is any space left in the townsman's permanent box, he should consult the seed or bedder lists (see pages 37, 41–5).

The rest of this chapter deals with colour schemes that have particularly pleased me.

The spring box

The colour schemes that follow may be introduced into the permanent box, or used for a complete planting of a spring box. In both cases the bulbs are put in during the autumn, and the carpet and spring bedding added in the early spring when it becomes available.

Bulbs are the making of the spring box and are discussed in Chapter 5; the spring bedders (see pages 13, 39) are their indispensable companions.

There are, to my mind, two spring bedders that should always be given a place: forget-me-nots and polyanthus. In my first book I included wallflowers, but, alas, I find they do not transplant easily in the spring, and winter losses in towns are often 10 per cent, so unwillingly I confine the wallflowers to autumn planting in the country box.

DAFFODIL ASSOCIATES

'Pheasant's Eye' Narcissi with blue primroses.

'King Alfred' with purple *Primula* 'Wanda'; a cheap mixture.

Narcissus 'Aranjuez', clear yellow perianth of perfect form with a shallow yellow crown deeply margined with orange-red; with wallflower 'Ivory White' (almost white).

White-trumpeted 'Beersheba' and gold-laced polyanthus: crimson edged with gold.

HYACINTH PARTNERS

White, cream, or pale pink hyacinths with dwarf forget-me-not 'Royal Blue'. This is my favourite mixture; or in reverse, pink forget-me-not 'Rose Gem' with pale blue hyacinth 'Myosotis'.

TULIP CONSORTS

Tulip 'Prince of Orange' carpeted with *Scilla sibirica*, or the improved *S. s.* 'Spring Beauty'.

Mixed double tulips and a carpet of chionodoxa.

Crocus, chionodoxa, grape hyacinth with the common primrose, in clumps or intermingled.

BEDDERS WITHOUT BULBS

Polyanthus, white, cream, yellow, and orange, of the Munstead strain, with the popular crimson.

The summer box

Here the choice is legion. First, I advise the inclusion of the summer flowerers given in the chapter on my favourites (page 91). They are antirrhinum, double daisy, campanula, dianthus, erigeron, fuchsia, geranium, iris, pansy, petunia, and viola. I confine further selection to bedding plants.

Begonia semperflorens (fibrous rooted). 9 in. First rate for edging the box. Only second to the geranium as the longest-flowering window box plant. Plumosa seedlings quickly mature. Young bedding plants usually available in late May. 'Pink Loveliness' is very profuse. June–October.

Celosia plumosa. Half-hardy annual 18 in. I was delighted to see this amusing plume-like flower proudly blooming last summer in the Government boxes of Whitehall. The cockscombs, red, orange, or yellow, measure from 9–12 in. long. This is not an easy flower to mix with others. The reds and scarlets look gay with fuchsias, the yellows show off well among the elegant grey foliage of *Centaurea candidissima*.

Coleus. Half-hardy perennial usually grown as an annual for its brilliant foliage. 2 ft. The variety usually grown has red leaves and golden markings, although there are more beautiful hybrids with deep purple leaves. It is interesting to note that the pinkish variety is free branching; the purple is not. This is a useful window box plant because of its spreading habit, but it requires a fine summer to succeed. It goes well with geraniums, among them scarlet 'Paul Crampel'. The likeable red-brown gold edge is known as 'Victoria' in the market.

Heliotrope. 2 ft. 'Cherry Pie' is a great bedding favourite, and 'The Speaker', a dark purple, is a particularly good and fragrant variety. Unfortunately, best colours have little scent. Conversely, 'Garfield' is not showy but is the best one for scent. Heliotropes are excellent mixers, either with petunias, annual phlox, blue salvia or with varieties of the Brompton stock, the rosy 'Empress Elizabeth' or 'White Lady'. 'Carmine King', is an outstanding drought-resister.

Lobelia. 6 in. The gardener should choose one of the more desirable varieties. 'Mrs Clibran Improved' has a bright blue flower with a captivating white eye. 'Sapphire' resembles it and hangs down gracefully over the front of the box. 'Rosamunde' is *vin rosé*. Light and dark blue flowers are effective blocked together, or form the gayest of edgings if not planted too far apart. Lobelias, petunias and white stocks make a lovely composition.

Pentstemon. 2 ft. The improved hybrids – crimson, scarlet and purple – are among the most brilliant summer bedders. They look dazzling with petunias. 'White Bedder' is an attractive variety that stands out well when carpeted with purple violas. 'Garnet' (Deep cerise), 'Ruby' (bright red), both hardy.

Phlox. *P. drummondii*, a half-hardy annual, 12 in., fits in with almost any colour scheme. There are splendid pink and red selfs, that mix admirably with rich-coloured pansies. *P. drummondii* var. *nana*, about 6 in., and the dwarf of the family, makes a good edging for the front of the box. These phloxes are excellent companions for lobelia, or the dwarf blue or mauve ageratum and will often flower for twelve weeks. *P. kermesina*, with white-centred carmine flowers that form a tight cluster, should not be missed out, while the new 'Twinkle' strain with gay star-flowers is bewitching.

Salvia. The red dazzlers so well known are varieties of *S. splendens*, such as 'Blaze of Fire'; there are also quieter pink varieties. Less strident are the blue varieties of *S. horminum* (a hardy annual), such as 'Blue Bird'. *S. patens* is a Cambridge-blue aristocrat, not densely flowered, that needs plenty of sun. Some gardeners like to interplant salvias with the 'Paris Daisy', the white marguerite. The blue salvias only require to be better known to become popular.

Stock. 15–24 in. Of the 'ten-week' summer stocks, 'Apple Blossom', rose tinted, 'Moonlight', pale yellow and 'Queen of the Whites' can always be recommended. 'Queen of the Whites' may be carpeted with viola 'Apricot Queen' or blue-black 'Velvet Monarch'.

Among the best of the 'giant perfection' varieties are 'Queen Alexandra', lilac-rose, 'Salmon King', 'Violette de Parme' and 'Capri', 'off-white', and rather a colour of its own.

Brompton stocks – sturdy, dense and colourful – bloom in April and May.

Tobacco plant. 12–18 in. The dwarf *Nicotiana* is an acquisition. Crimson and white 'Beddus' should be given a trial. Seedlings are usually cheap and available.

Tobacco plants with fuchsias or heliotrope standards make a delightful display. They have now been bred to remain with flowers open during the day.

Verbena. 9–15 in. Red, pink, mauve, purple or white. I can recommend 'Lawrence Johnson', a crimson-red; it is a brilliant variety. Some of the hybrids are semi-prostrate and are helpful in disguising the shortcomings of a neighbour – a leggy pentstemon or overgrown stock.

Bright yellow antirrhinums and pink verbenas or dark-red intermediate antirrhinums and white or pink dwarf verbenas make a splash of colour.

Zinnia. 15–30 in. These plants have been tremendously improved during the last years, and there are mammoth varieties that are as large as the smaller types of dahlia, as well as accommodating dwarfs. Flowers are to be had in almost any shade. When deciding upon the colour scheme, remember that the zinnia is a late-summer flowerer and can be madly temperamental. It must have full sun.

The most successful window box of zinnias that I have seen was one of mixed varieties carpeted with white alyssum. The Lilliput group, seldom more than 12 in. high, show up well when interplanted with silver-leaved *Centaurea*, while the fascinating 'Thumbelina' is only 4 in.

The autumn window box often fails to get its share of thought, all enthusiasm and funds having been spent on the summer display.

The following four plants play an important part during the autumn months.

Aster. The dwarf Michaelmas Daisies need no further description, although some gardeners are still unaware of the many new groups and beautiful varieties; the dwarfs are ideal for the window box and have already been recommended for the permanent box (page 74). They can be intermingled with *Sedum spectabile* or late-flowering *Lobelia syphilitica* or pink *Oxalis floribunda*.

A. amellus is about 2 ft high, compact and with large flowers, is also invaluable. 'King George' is a first-rate violet-blue, and there is a series of good pinks, among them 'Sonia', a bright rose.

China aster. (*Callistephus chinensis*, not really an Aster.) 10–36 in. Few gardeners can afford to overlook the China aster; mauve, white, or pink, single or double. It is best bought as a seedling about May. The 'Aurora' or Anemone-flowered can be had in a wide range of colours. The Lilliputs make neat bedders, and the Ray asters, with finely quilled florets, are considered to possess a little more quality than their relations. Newcomers appear in the catalogues every year. Single pink China asters backed by blue or white asters make a good mixture.

Chrysanthemum. 2 ft upwards. The autumn box may contain one or two perennial border chrysanthemums of the *C. morifolium* and *C. rubellum* type. It should also include representatives from the Korean branch of the family, the single-flowered hybrids. These, though best wintered inside, are exceptionally hardy.

The yellow chrysanthemums mix well with the white anemones, the pink-shaded varieties should be planted among the asters. The favourite yellow chrysanth for window boxes is 'Denise', which has taken the place of 'Jante Wells'.

The gardener who returns home from holiday and finds his box in a poor state has at this time of year little choice: he may take the easy way and replace with pompons.

Dahlia. 15–18 in. The Mignon single-flowered dahlia that blooms so freely is an admirable autumn bedding plant.

Coltness 'Gem Improved' is a bright red, and a more consistent flowerer than the original scarlet bedder from which it was raised. It stands out well when planted with white Mignon varieties such as 'Innocence', white anemones, small white asters, or late-flowering white violas. 'Pride of Edentown', a double crimson scarlet on strong stems rising above dark green foliage, can be brought into the same composition, and with crimson-red 'Maureen Creighton', another sturdy plant with possibly vermilion 'Corona', will provide a splendid box of mixed reds. Nothing is more telling than a box of different shaded scarlets, reds, and crimsons. 'Pink Gem', an outstanding pink variety, should be found a place among the pale-shaded asters.

These four plants are helpful in prolonging the flowering season; the new and improved varieties have a much extended flowering period and now bloom from July until the frost is in the air.

The one-flower box with two varieties

Spring

CROCUS. Sutton's Lilac-veined with Sutton's Deep Purple.

FORGET-ME-NOT. Barr's 'Alpine Blue' with 'Royal Blue', or either of these intermingled with any pink or white variety. Plant in the spring with a little sharp sand round the collar of the plant.

SCILLA. Bluebell. *S. campanulata* 'Alba', white, with either 'Blue Queen' or 'Rose Queen'. These are enchanting arrangements.

Summer.

ANTIRRHINUM. 'Wisley', 'Golden Fleece', with 'Orange Glow'.

BEGONIA. 'Black Knight', deep crimson, with 'Estella Jowell', white; or 'Mary Kirton', orange-apricot, with 'Mildred Butler', cream-primrose.

FUCHSIA. 'Tom Thumb', light crimson sepals and purple corolla, with *F. pumila*, small scarlet and mauve flowers. Both these plants are miniatures.

GERANIUM (properly, *Pelargonium*). 'Nanette', a soft salmon pink, a beautiful single with a pronounced white eye, with Tresor, a delicate salmon white-striped. These plants are not always easily obtained. If the gardener has the opportunity, he should visit the growers and choose his varieties.

I have a vivid memory of a box of salmon and apricots that I saw in America. This is a favourite colour scheme in the States.

Different shades of magenta make a striking box. Among these there are 'A. M. Mayne', 'Dagata', 'Dublin' and 'Emil David'.

Of the choice ivy-leaf group, 'Leopard', a lilac-pink with crimson blotched upper petals, is a splendid mixer and looks particularly delightful with lilac 'Lord Baden-Powell' or 'La France'.

'Eclipse', a pink that is an improvement on 'Madame Crousse,' goes well with 'Galilee', the double rose; these two are reasonably priced and usually available.

Lastly, I hope I will be forgiven for putting in a word for my namesake 'Xenia Field' geranium, a zonal, biscuit-pink with a phlox-like eye.

HELIOTROPE. Any two varieties of the *Heliotropium* available. 'The Speaker' and 'Sir Edward Fry' are dark violet, and there is always free-flowering 'Lord Roberts', which is a lighter shade of violet and deliciously fragrant. These can be put alongside lilac-blue 'Madame Cellier', or rosy-coloured 'Swanley Giant'. Plants trained as standard are effective, rising above bedding plants.

VERBENA. Purple and lavender or pink and red varieties.

From seed

CANDYTUFT. 'Rose Cardinal', a rosy-scarlet, sown with a packet of crimson, lilac or purple seed. Or 'White Rocket' with pink seed. The 'Iberis' is indifferent to poor soil, and is one of the easiest annuals to grow. Seedlings should be well thinned out.

CORNFLOWER. 'Jubilee Gem', a double free-flowerer with 'Rose Gem', its pink counterpart. These are compact growers only 12 in. high. There are many new shades of the centaurea worth consideration, most of them semi-doubles.

NASTURTIUM. The *Tropaeolum* (the correct generic name) is probably the best-known town annual. 'Orange' with 'Scarlet Gleam' makes a dashing mixture, or 'Wallflower Gleam' a mahogany red, with 'Orange Gleam'. There are many new shades in the 'Tom Thumbs'; the primrose and cherry varieties are pretty together.

Autumn

ASTER (Michaelmas Daisy). Dwarf aster 'Rose Bonnet', soft pink, with Snowsprite, a pure white semi-double. Both about 9 in. high and flowering from September onwards; they are easy to please and most rewarding.

CHINA ASTER. Any two colours of Carter's Giant Singles. Mauve, deep mauve, white, pink and scarlet.

CHRYSANTHEMUM (dwarf varieties). 'Hebe', pink and white, with 'Vulcan', crimson.

DAHLIA. 'Busby Gem', a single rich deep yellow, with 'Diamond', a single orange-buff.

The two-flower box

This appears to be the most popular composition.

Spring

NARCISSUS. 'Cheerfulness', the double-flowered creamy-white narcissus with a yellow centre that has three or four flowers on a stem, with red-purple *Primula* 'Wanda'.

'*Actaea*', the true, scented Poet's Narcissus that has a large white flower with a scarlet-rimmed eye, with yellow and white polyanthus of the Giant Munstead strain or Carter's Sunset hybrids of orange, tangerine, and buff (from which the scarlets and dark reds have been eliminated).

'Golden Harvest', a yellow trumpet of great size and splendid substance, with Carter's Prize Gold-Edged polyanthus; the flowers are edged and laced with gold.

PRIMULA. *P. auricula* 'Argus' with the wallflowers apricot 'Eastern Queen', ruby-red 'Ellen Willmott', or 'Primrose Monarch'.

TULIP. Vermilion. Brilliant carpeted with ultramarine *Scilla sibirica*.

ANTIRRHINUM. 'Wisley Golden Fleece' with *Calendula* 'Orange King', the double-flowered marigold, 15 in. high and an intense showy orange.

Antirrhinum Pink 'Wisley Bridesmaid' with mignonette 'Bismarck'.

BEGONIA. Scarlet 'Caroline Coe' carpeted with 'Crystal Palace', the dark blue lobelia.

FUCHSIA. Rose of Castile, white and purple, with white marguerites.

GERANIUM (Pelargonium). Bright pink 'Madame Crousse' with *Campanula poscharskayana* 'Alba'. The popular scarlet 'Paul Crampel' (tall or standard plants) with a background of white tobacco 'Daylight': only 18 in.

Deep cherry 'Charles Turner' with Brompton stocks, pale rose-pink or rich dark violet.

'Galilee', the pink ivy-leaved geranium, with 'Sapphire', the trailing deep blue lobelia with a white eye.

GODETIA. Dwarf salmon or dwarf lavender or mauve with white verbena.

HELIOTROPE. 'Mrs J. W. Lowther', a violet bedder of repute, with 'Pink Freedom', a pink buff antirrhinum. Small plants are effective when planted with the dwarf blue ageratum, or *Phlox drummondii*, or a good strain of pansy, such as yellow 'Winter Sun', that has a fascinating dark eye.

Lastly, heliotrope and purple verbena, whatever their variety, show each other off to advantage.

LOBELIA. 'Blue Gown' lobelia and 'Little Blue Star' ageratum make a modest box of great charm. Lobelia with London Pride. Lobelia must be thickly planted to be effective.

MARIGOLD. This annual shows off well among yellow marguerites or annual chrysanthemums; deep golden-yellow chrysanthemum 'Evening Star', or the more delicate sulphur-yellow 'Morning Star', are bright among the marigolds.

PETUNIA. Dwarfs 'Blue Prince' or 'Rose Queen' are satisfactory companions for the double Indian Pinks, or they can be planted with violas, or *Anchusa capensis* 'Blue Bird', 18 in., indigo blue.

SALVIA. The blue *S. pratensis* 'Tenoril' carpeted with *Campanula poscharsky-ana* 'Alba'.

STOCK. 'White Snowdrift' with 'King of the Blacks' pansy.

From seed

CANDYTUFT. Rich purple patterned with carmine and lilac varieties, with the dwarf cornflower 'Rose Gem'.

NASTURTIUMS. Dwarfs in front, semi-double 'Gleams' at the back, trained upwards.

Autumn

DWARF ASTER. 'Nancy', pink, or 'Victor', lavender, with the elegant grey-foliaged *Centaurea argentea*.

CHRYSANTHEMUM. The Korean hybrids, 'Orion', a canary yellow, or 'The Moor', a double wine-red, with white China asters.

DAHLIA. 'Pink Pearl', a double rosy pink, with the dwarf aster 'Venus', bright pink, or 'Blue Bird', violet-blue.

The country box

Maybe the gardener is a country enthusiast who has been obliged to live in the city. The less sophisticated flowers can also wave in the city breeze, and even buttercups and daisies are found a place. A box of this kind can have great charm, but the natural planting and arrangements demanded by wild inconspicuous flowers are not easily achieved. These are a few of my favourites.

FLOWERS

Anemone
Bluebell
Bugle
Celandine
Cornflower
Cowslip
Daisy
Geranium
Harebell (*Campanula rotundifolia*)
Lady's Smock

Loosestrife
Mallow
Marguerite
Mouse-ear Hawkweeds
Orchid (native terrestrial species, e.g. *Orchis purpurea*)
Poppy
Primrose
Ragged Robin
Red Campion
Violet

GRASSES

Briza minor (or *minima*), the quaking grass; 6 in.
Dactylis glomerata elegantissima. Variegated cock's-foot grass, silver and green. 9 in.
Festuca glauca. Bluish-grey, of erect habit. 6 in.

The fodder plants of the clover family should be considered, and the small hardy ferns found a place where there are boxes in the shade.

The box in the sun

Most plants like to bask in the sun, but the following plants seem to enjoy it even more than their fellows:

Alyssum	*Cotyledon*	Nasturtium
Armeria (Thrift)	Creeping Jenny	*Scabiosa*
Aster	*Gazania*	Sedum
Aubrieta	Geranium	*Sempervivum*
Campanula	Iris	Zinnia
Carnation	Mesembryanthemum	
Chrysanthemum	Mignonette	

Gazanias, zinnias and mesembryanthemums in particular should have the utmost possible sun.

The box in partial shade

There are a number of plants that will grow in partial shade:

Antirrhinum	*Hermerocallis* (Day Lily)	Pansy
Aster	*Heuchera*	*Polygonatum*
Begonia	*Iberis*	Primula
Calceolaria	Iris (bulbous)	Saxifrages
Campanula	Japanese Anemone	(including
Corydalis	Lily of the Valley	London Pride)
Creeping Jenny	*Lunaria* (Honesty)	Sedum
Dielytra (Dicentra)	*Lythrum*	*Sempervivum*
Dictamnus	*Meconopsis*	Solidago
Doronicum	*Myosotis*	*Thalictrum*
Fuchsia	Nasturtium	*Trillium*
Geum	Night-scented Stock	Viola

Some Colour Scheme Suggestions:

Antirrhinum, candytuft and pansies.
Auriculas and forget-me-nots.
Fuchsias and violas.
Nasturtiums and creeping jenny.
Night-scented stock and pansies.

The box in full shade

This is a bad business. Plants will grow in the shade, but they are shy of flowering. The following do their best:

Anemone japonica.
Antirrhinum 'Asarina'. Yellow, trailing.
Cerastium.
Epimedium 'Bishop's Hat'
Ferns (hardy).
Funkia (*Hosta*).
Hedera (Ivy) (see page 111).
Helleborus.
Honesty.
Hypericum
Iris (bulbous).
Lamium galeobdolon. Yellow. Rapid ground cover.
L. maculata 'Chequers'. Improved form, deep pink flowers.
Lily of the Valley.
Linaria (Toad flax).
Nepeta (catmint).
Night-scented stock.
Polygonatum (Solomon's Seed).
Saxifraga umbrosa (London Pride).
Tiarella.
Vinca major (Periwinkle): Gold (ideal with ferns).
V. minor variegata: gold, also silver forms.

GREENHOUSE PLANTS USEFUL AS SUMMER BEDDING-OUT PLANTS

Coleus.
Helxine.
Impatiens (Busy Lizzie).

Plumbago capensis.
Tradescantia (Wandering Jew).

FERNS

Hardy ferns have come back into favour and can be combined with creeping jenny for a happy mixture. They must be given plenty of leaf and peat mould and regular watering.

Mr H. Taylor, an expert on this subject, has suggested the following ferns for the north or shaded window box.

Athyrium filix-femina cristatum. Crested Lady Fern. Great delicacy of design. Fronds are killed by severe frost but bright green lace and frills return in the spring.

Cystopteris bulbifera. A North American fern that grown to 6–18 in.

Dryopteris linnaeana. Oak Fern. Demands complete shade. Difficult and prefers country conditions.

Phyllitis scolopendrium. The common Harts-tongue fern, and the willing *P. s. chrispatum* both bravely survive a London basement.

P. s. chrispatum. Crested Harts-tongue fern, demanding kinder conditions.

Polystichum setiferum acutilobum (proliferum). The largest on the list: a semi-horizontal grower.

The foliage box

Beautiful box arrangements can be made from some plants whose chief attraction is in their foliage – smooth or rough-leaved, dense and impenetrable or almost transparent, often highly coloured, as in the *Coleus*, or silvery-white, as in the next section.

Centaurea rutifolia (candidissima). Silver foliage, bedding plant.

Coleus. White, purple, bronze, and red foliage.

Ferns. See Mr Taylor's selections in the previous section.

Funkia (or *Hosta*). Many species have leaves edged silvery-white, blotched with white, golden-leaved, creamy white, and greyish-green or blue.

Geranium. Many 'geraniums' are grown for the beauty of their variegated foliage alone. The flowers incline to be insignificant and can be picked off.

SELECTIONS:

'Crystal Palace Gem'. Yellow leaf with green markings.

'Flower of Spring'. Silver leaf.

'Happy Thought'. Variegated. Soft green; yellow butterfly markings.

'His Majesty'. Variegated.
'Lady Churchill'. Silver leaf.
'Mrs Quilter'. Golden-bronze.
'Mrs Harvey Cox'. Finest golden and red tricolour.
'Mrs Mapping'. Silver leaf.
'Mrs Pollock'. The golden tricolour veteran.
'Marshall McMahon'. Rich bronze tricolour.
'Verona'. Pure yellow leaf. Excellent with dark foliage.

Helxine soleirolii. Known as 'Mind your own Business'. Neat bright green leaves with creeping and trailing shoots. An invasive weed in the open garden, but a white house decorated with window boxes of *Helxine* looks elegant. The new *aurea* or golden variety is superb.

Kochia. A foliage plant, resembling a dwarf cypress; apple-green in summer. then purple-red. 2 ft.

Sagina subulata. (Pearlwort). A moss-like weed in the open garden, but the golden-leaved variety, 'Aurea', can be used for carpet bedding. It has the unfortunate habit of dying off in patches and must be constantly renewed.

The grey and silver foliage box

The flower arranger discovered the value of grey foliage and has encouraged the nurseryman to propagate silver and grey leaved plants. These give a window box a great air of distinction. They are almost without exception sun lovers, capable of standing a certain amount of damp but resent wet conditions. The grey and silver foliage box flourishes on walls facing south, south-east, or west, but *not* north. Some of the plants, such as *Artemisia glacialis*, are not sufficiently hardy to stand up to frost until well established and are for this reason better planted in mid-May.

Mrs Desmond Underwood of Ramparts Nurseries, Colchester. specialises in grey and silver foliage plants, and displays them along with the hardy hybrid pinks. The shrimp-pink, red-eyed 'Doris' is an outstanding pink for this purpose and none is more free-flowering, but I am particularly fond of 'Prudence', a veteran with a white ground and distinct crimson lacing.

The grey foliage plants vary in price, but the majority of them and the pinks are to be had for about 50p each. Here is my selection for the box.

Achillea argentea. Rosettes of small silver white leaves; 6 in. *A.* 'Peter Davies'. Very tough; 6 in.

1 Fuchsias and geraniums

2 A diversity of petunias

Anaphalis nubigena. Grey foliage; clusters of pearly immortelle flowers in August; 12 in.

Anthemis rudolphiana. Feathery silver leaved foliage: bright yellow flower end of May. The anthemis is best cut down after flowering, enabling the plant to make some new growth before the colder weather; 9 in.

Artemisia glacialis. A pure silver rockery plant that pokes its nose through the snow; 2 in.

A. lanata. A moss-like form of the family.

A. pedemontana. A shrublet; 4 in.

A. schmidtii nana. Silver cushions that turn russet red in the autumn; 7 in. Beware sparrows.

Centaurea maritima. With felted white leaves: tender and will not over-winter outside; 12 in.

Chrysanthemum poterifolium. Rockery tough, very white in winter. Usually over-winters; 4 in.

Convolvulus cneorum. Handsome but tender – a crevice plant.

Helichrysum italicum. Miniature Curry plant – will make a clipped hedge for the back of the box; 12 in.

Lavandula lanata. Attractive but not hardy lavender. For the well-drained box. White sweetly scented flowers; 7 in.

Santolina incana var. 'Weston'. The woolliest member of the cotton lavender family: 18 in. across: 9 in. height.

Stachys lanata. Lamb's lugs or Sow's ears, with grey-white nap foliage; has been a cottager's favourite for centuries. Should be replanted every second year; 12 in.

Teucrium polium. White-leaved rockery plant that keeps its foliage through the winter. Neat; 4 in.

Thymus citriodorus. The lemon-scented variegated thyme. Cushion shaped; 8–12 in.

Veronica 'Wendy'. Grey leaves, violet flowers; 10 in.

V. cineraria azurea. A fast-growing carpet plant that must be cut back after flowering if it is to develop its attractive white shoots; height 4 in.

Mrs Desmond Underwood has chosen ten suitable plants for an *almost* hardy grey and silver box:

2 *Helichrysum plicatum* 'Elmstead'. Small growing and very white.
2 Doris pinks, quite hardy.
2 *Helichrysum petiolatum* for trailing. These are not hardy and must be

found a sunny window-sill indoors for the winter. They are excellent for spring cutting; 3 in.

2 *Artemisia splendens*, 18 in.; 'a froth of silver'.

1 *Artemisia lanata pedemontana*.

1 *Tanecetum densum amanum*.

Mrs Underwood has two *Senecio* 'White Diamond' in her own window box. She prunes them heavily in late April, but one, a veteran, has developed a heavy trunk and its loving owner doubts whether she will be able to keep it much longer.

Tanecetum densum amanum makes a carpet of little Prince of Wales plumes.

15 Some of my Favourites

Gardeners love roses – almost to a man – but beyond this no two seem to love alike. So in this book I have given various lists of various sorts for various people, hoping that everybody will find something to please him. Perhaps the reader may care to consider those plants that I have found to be the best value.

Antirrhinum. (Snapdragon.) Perennial. Loses appearance after second year. Best treated as annual. Various colours and heights. Plant well-hardened plants April–May. Good loam. Easy but tendency to rust disease. Rust-free strains recommended. Sunny position or partial shade. Pinch out leading shoot to make bushy and longer flowering.

Varieties: The following are 'Intermediates', height 15–18 in. and rust-resistant:
'Wisley Bridesmaid'. Pink.
'Wisley Cheerful'. Pink suffused golden.
'Wisley Golden Fleece'. Sulphur yellow.
'Orange Glow'. Deep orange with cerise throat. One of the brightest flowers.
'Pink Freedom'. Rich terracotta on buff.
The dwarf or 'Little Gem' hybrids, 4–6 in., are worth consideration.

Aubrieta. Spreading evergreen perennial, 3–6 in. Mauve, pink, and crimson. April–May. Plant spring or autumn. Ordinary good soil. Propagation: divide in spring or autumn; a rooted sprig is ideal. Cut back after flowering; top dress with compost.

Varieties

'Barker's Double'. Large crimson, almost double. Effective.
'Carnival'. Purple. Early.
'Crimson Queen'. Bright red.
'Dr Mules'. Violet-purple. Old and valued friend.

'J. S. Baker'. Showy violet-blue: white eye.
'Magnificent'. Large rosy-crimson. Vigorous.
'Mrs Rodewald'. The best red.
'Purple Splendour'. Deepest purple.
'*Rosea splendens*'. Pink, Pleasant. Profuse.

Aubrietas are also very easily raised from seed. A packet will give you dozens of plants, in various colours.

Begonia. Most are tuberous-rooted perennials. Various colours. July–October. Start tubers March–April in shallow box filled rich light soil. Lay tubers close together near surface, concave side up, crowns uncovered. Keep in a warm dark place, watering sparingly until growth active. When shoots are one inch high pot up, adding sprinkling of bonemeal to compost. Once growing water generously. Remove early buds. When reaching flowering stage, fortnightly doses of liquid manure appreciated. Protect from full sun. Remove plants end October before danger of frost. Stand in tray to dry, then shake off the soil; examine for decay. Cut away any rot, dust with powdered charcoal. Store for winter in cool, frost-proof place; temperature not above 50°F (10°C) or tubers will shrivel.

Varieties: These can be bought reasonably under colour headings – singles, doubles, fringed, and crested. There are also small unnamed collections sold by specialists. Mr Bryan Langdon of Blackmore & Langdon's names six desirables of the cheaper named varieties:

'Aurora'. Salmon-orange.
'Clouded'. Yellow, lightly tinted orange. Free flowering.
'Everest'. White.
'H. Frankling'. Rich vermilion.
'John Langdon'. Salmon-rose.
'N. F. Barnes'. Large rich orange.

The brilliant dwarf begonia, in red, pink, or white, used for bedding schemes is *B. semperflorens*, which is fibrous-rooted.

Bellis. *Bellis perennis plena* is the perennial double daisy or Hen and Chickens, in pink, red, or white. April–July; 3–5 in. Plant early spring. Ordinary soil. Propagation: division after summer flowering. No particular tastes. Mixes admirably with spring bulbs. Plant 3 in. apart. Flowers months on end for almost anybody.

'Alice'. Salmon-pink.   'White Globe'.
'Dresden China'. Pink.   'Rob Roy'. Red, quilled.
'Miniature Dresden'. White.

Campanula. The bell flower or harebell. A large family, some growing
5 ft high, but we are concerned here with the alpine dwarfs in blue, mauve,
or white. Plant spring or autumn. Sunny crevice or partial shade.

Species

C. isophylla. Pale mauve. Modest, charming, rather tender. 6 in. July–August.
C. poscharskyana. Trailing and very vigorous. Grey-blue; 3–4 in. Summer.
C. p. 'Alba'. White form.

Chrysanthemum. Perennial; colours various; late summer and autumn;
plant spring; ordinary rich soil. Propagation by division and cuttings from
young basal shoots in spring. Sunny position. Well decayed manure usefully
worked into soil in spring; fortnightly doses liquid manure until flower buds
form.

Hardy chrysanths make a good-natured tray planting if introduced in the
spring and the tray returned to the garden in October.

Obviously, we are not here concerned with the splendours of the show
bench or the florist's shop, but with those of more modest stature. The following
selection of suitable varieties (height up to 18 in.) has been made by specialist
Laurence W. Neel.

DWARF CUSHION TYPES

'Golden Anemone'. Golden apricot, 18 in.
'Pastel Blanket'. Chamois, 6–9 in.
'Primrose Anemone'. Soft yellow, 18 in.
'Scarleteer'. Bright red, 18 in.
'Sea Urchin'. Lemon white, 12 in.
'Snowbound'. White, 18 in.

HARDY POMS

'Baby Tears'. Pure white cushion, 12 in.
'Browneyes'. Golden orange, 15 in.
'Denise'. Yellow, 12 in. (has ousted 'Jante Wells').
'Grandchild'. Mauve pink, 12–18 in.

HARDY BORDER VARIETIES (Koreans). Many of the shorter Korean varieties are suitable. Beware of slugs in spring, and protect during a very hard winter. if left in the box to over-winter. Otherwise, plant in early spring and once established feed with liquid manure once every ten days until the buds begin to colour.

Mr John Woolman kindly reminds me that the new Perpetuals, height 6–12 in., and flowers 4 in. across, in white, pink, or yellow, and the new race of Dwarf Lilliputs, 8–12 in. with double flowers, are very suitable for the window box.

Dahlia. Half-hardy, tuberous-rooted perennial. Colours and heights various. July until frost. Plant out early June; good rich compost. Dahlias are thirsty and greedy. Propagation is by division of crowns in spring or by spring cuttings with heel. Glasshouse or frame desirable. Plant the small bedders 18 in. apart. Regular watering is important; fortnightly applications of liquid manure are helpful. Dead heads must be cut. Lift after first frost; dry, clean, cutting down to within 6 in. of tuber. Place in box lightly covered with dry peat or coconut fibre. If the tubers are kept plump, young shoots will appear early the following year and provide useful cuttings.

Varieties: The following are chosen by the well-known dahlia expert, Mr Stuart Ogg:

'Butter Ball'. Miniature dwarf bedding, rich yellow, $1\frac{1}{2}$ ft.
'Corona'. Small semi-cactus, vermillion with yellow base, 2 ft.
'Dazzler'. Miniature dwarf bedder, bright scarlet with yellow base, 2 ft.
'Park Princess'. Semi-cactus dwarf bedder, pale pink, 2 ft.
'Piper's Pink'. Small semi-cactus, deep pink excellent for tubs, $2\frac{1}{2}$ ft.
'Red Flash'. Single dwarf bedder, scarlet with dark foliage, $1\frac{1}{2}$ ft.

The Lilliput Dahlias, growing to only a foot or so in height and with flowers measuring between 1 and $1\frac{1}{2}$ in. in diameter, are delightful for window boxes They need no support, but must be carefully dead-headed.

Philip Damp, secretary of the National Dahlia Society, names his choice of varieties:

'Chessy'. Bronze and yellow blends.
'Dandy'. Purple with dark foliage.
'Exotic Dwarf'. Pink with a darker ring.
'Ino'. Light yellow.
'Lemon'. Clear lemon.
'Omo'. Pure white.

'Pinnochio'. Ruby red with a bronze centre.
'Red Dwarf'. Bright red with darker centre.

Dianthus. I have chosen these few from a large family which includes the carnation, pink and Sweet William. July–August. They tend to grow leggy and a good supply of cuttings and layers is desirable.

CARNATION. Perennial; various colours. Summer. They like a good turf loam, with rotted manure, river sand, plenty of limestone or mortar rubble. Protect cuttings and layers against strong sun until established.

Varieties: The following are chosen for their well-formed, good-stemmed flowers, tidy habit and sound calyx by Mr John Galbally, the hardy border carnation specialist.

'Golden Cross'. Bright yellow self.
'Kathleen Hitchcock'. Deep pink self.
'Maudie Hinds'. Bright yellow splashed scarlet.
'Maureen Saunders'. White feathered rose.
'Sandra Neal'. Apricot flaked deep pink.
'Whitesmith'. Pure white self.

PINKS. These may be annuals or perennials in crimson, white, mauve or pink. June–July. Culture as for carnations but soil less rich.

Species and Varieties

D. *chinensis* (or *heddewigii*). Chinese or Indian Pink. An annual usually pink
  and red with frilled edges. 9 in. July–October. Best bought as bedding plant.
D. *plumarius*. 'Earl of Sussex', pink, crimson marking. 'Mrs Sinkins'; white
  and of great fame. 'White Ladies'; the best white. 8–12 in.

Erigeron. Fleabane. Perennial. Dwarf forms in various colours. Daisy-like, free flowering. Not unlike Michaelmas Daisy. Plant spring or autumn; ordinary soil. Propagation: division in spring or autumn.

E. *mucronatus* is a charming little pink and white daisy of 5 in. with thin foliage, easy from seed. 'Four Winds' is a 4 in. pink.

Fuchsia. Deciduous shrub, with summer flowers in blue, red, pink, purple and white. Plant out the harf-hardy in June and the hardy in spring. Soil: two parts fibrous loam, one part leaf-mould and sprinkling sharp sand. Semi-shady position best facing east or north. Propagation: by cuttings, the hardy in July–August and the half-hardies from new 4–5 in. shoots in March. All are vulnerable to severe frost; give protection with ashes or dry litter after pruning to strong shoots or right to the base. Water generously in spring and summer. Weekly doses liquid manure beneficial before flowering. In September gradually withhold water; lift during the third week and store in a frost-proof place. In winter keep dry but not arid. In February pot up again. Water sparingly until in full growth. Plant out the first week of June.

Hardy Species

F. gracilis. Scarlet sepals; single, good spreading habit.
F. pumila. Scarlet and mauve; a miniature, single.

Half-hardy Varieties

'Marinka'. Tube and sepals crimson-scarlet, velvety red corolla. Medium-sized flowers; profuse. Single.
'Rose of Castille' Improved. Flesh-coloured sepals, violet-purple corolla; vigorous. Single.
'Tom Thumb'. Tub and sepals scarlet-cerise, mauve corolla, 1 ft.

The late Mr Tom Thorn, a fuchsia specialist, gave me the following choices for the window-box:

Hardy Varieties

'Mrs Popple'. Scarlet sepals; rich purple corolla.
'Madame Cornelissen'. Scarlet tube and sepal, white corolla.

Half-hardy Varieties. Four for a box – two upright and two to fall over the box:

'Citation'. Light cerise sepals, the large corolla is white veined cerise and flared. Upright. A beautiful American and my favourite fuchsia.
'Flying Cloud'. Creamy white self with a touch of pink in the centre. Upright.
'Aunt Juliana'. Pale red tube and sepals, pastel blue corolla. Trailer.
'Angel's Flight'. Flesh pink sepals, long white tube. Double corolla with white centre sepals and short side-skirt petals. Thrives in basket or box.

Mr Thorn stressed the point that the fuchsia will die on you if allowed to dry out completely during the winter. It must be kept partially dry, but *never* desert dry.

Mr E. J. Wills of West Wittering, Chichester, known for his striking displays at the Chelsea Show, names his choice for the window box:

'Achievement'. Single, cerise sepals, magenta corolla. Large, well-shaped.
'Heidi Ann'. Double, crimson tube, pale orchid purple corolla. (Medium sized, free flowering.)

96

'Leonora'. The best single pink, perfect shaped corolla.
'Marin Glow'. Single, pure waxy-white sepals, rich purple corolla. Distinctive.
'White Ann'. Double, crimson sepals, white corolla.
'W. Churchill'. Double, pink sepals, silvery-blue corolla. Free and shapely.

For tubs:

'Tolling Bells'. Single, scarlet tube and sepals, white corolla.
'Royal Velvet'. Double, crimson sepals, deep purple corolla.
'J. Acland'. Single, bright pink sepals, pink corolla. Free.

For baskets:

'Red Spider'. Single, deep crimson sepals, dark rose corolla.
'Cascade'. Single, white sepals, flushed carmine, deep carmine corolla. Cascading.

Helleborus (Christmas Rose.) Perennial. White, pink, or green. Plant spring or early autumn. Rich leafy loam. Propagation: by division in spring. Enjoys semi-shade; resents hot sun. Keep moist in summer. Mulch with well-decayed manure in early spling. Resents disturbance.

Species: *H. niger*. The well-known white Christmas Rose, 1 ft April–May; and *H. orientalis*. Lenten Rose, purple, pink, white. 2 ft.

Ipomoea. (Morning Glory), closely related to convolvulus. Half-hardy annual and climber. Wide funnel-shaped flower, usually blue. One of the most beautiful climbers. Reasonable soil. Water freely once established and growing. Best bought as bedder from seeds sown in warm greenhouse in spring. Rather tender and should not be planted earlier than June. Takes ten weeks from seed to flower. Suggest seed should be soaked five hours in luke warm water before sowing. Young plants available at stores and markets. The usual one is *I. rubro-coerula*, a superb, intense blue.

Iris. I mention irises several times in this book, but here I want specially to recommend *I. pumila*, a miniature 'flag' of 6 in. stature, flowering in the spring. Unlike those in Chapter 5, it is not a bulb, but roots from a rhizome (Chapter 18). It deserves wider popularity. Plant in early summer or after flowering in rich loam with lime or mortar rubble added. *No manure*. Propagate as in Chapter 18. The species has several colour forms: *I. pumila* 'Blue Pigmy'; *I. p. cyanea*, pfile blue; *I. p. lutea*, yellow; and 'The Bride', silvery-white, 1 ft.

Pelargonium. The petunia is the eye-catcher, but the VIP of the box is the geranium, or, more correctly the Pelargonium. This is a half-hardy perennial from South Africa, with flowers in pink, red, white or mauve. The zonal group, so called from their circular markings on green scalloped leaves, is best suited for the window box. Plant out early in June in two parts good fibrous loam, with half a part well-decayed stable manure and a small addition of bonemeal. A nitrogenous feed often leads to excessive foliage and few flowers.

Bring indoors before there is a danger of frost. Pot up or put in a box and store in a cool frost-proof place for the winter. The temperature must not fall below 40 °F (4½° C). Water only to avoid desert-dryness until the spring.

Next year, wait for the plants to wake up, then cut them back hard and re-pot. Old misshapen plants are unattractive. Firm planting and good balanced feeding are essential. Fertiliser is much appreciated.

PROPAGATION: cuttings are best taken August to October. Firm shoots 3-4 in. long cleanly cut just below third or fourth joint are those wanted. Avoid sappy stems with large leaves. Remove lower leaves and stipules (small leaf-appendages). Veteran gardeners wait to insert the cuttings until two days later, so that the wound has time to callous, but modern gardeners prefer to dip the cutting in a 'hormone' rooting powder and to plant straightaway. Beware of damping-off. Water only when dry. Pinch out the tips of the growing shoots early and so promote bushy growth.

The geranium was Queen Victoria's pride; it has taken on new life since being disassociated from lobelia. Too often neglected, gardeners traded on the plant's good nature.

SPECIES AND VARIETIES

Zonal Pelargoniums

'Dot Slade'. Single salmon with deeper-shaded veins. Free.

'Festiva Maxima'. The finest purple. Double.

'Gustave Emich'. Large, beautiful, semi-double scarlet.

'Ryecroft White'. Double.

'Willingdon Gem'. Single salmon; large white eye.

'Decorator'. Single scarlet.

'King of Denmark'. Semi-double; salmon pink.

'Maxim Kovalevski'. Single orange. Strong plant when happy!

'Orangesonne'. Double. Brilliant orange that may well oust Crampel and Emich.

'Paul Crampel'. Single scarlet. Magnificent doer. Madly popular.

'Queen of Denmark'. Semi-double salmon. Improvement on the King in colour. Not quite as tough.

'Xenia Field'. Biscuit-pink, white eye.

Scented-leaved Species. Grown for their fragrant foliage.

P. crispum variegatum. Variegated silver small leaves: lemon-scented.
P. fragrans. Sage green; silver sheen. Orange-scented.
P. tomentosum. Flat velvety leaves; peppermint-scented.

Variegated-leaved Varities. The flowers are usually unimportant and some
gardeners pick them off.

'Crystal Palace Gem'. Yellow leaf; green markings.
'Lady Churchill' (synonym, 'Chelsea Gem'). Silver.
'Mr Henry Cox'. Probably the brightest tricolour; gold bronze, red, and
   cream.
'Mrs Pollock'. Golden veteran.

Ivy-leaved Varieties

The gardener is advised to send for a pelargonium specialist's catalogue and
to break fresh ground. Here are some suggestions:

'Abel Carrière'. Double purplish magenta.
'Charles Turner'. Pink, feathered maroon.
'Eclipse'. Pink; improvement on 'Madame Crousse'.
'Galilee'. The popular rose pink.
'Mauve Galilee'. Charming newcomer.
'La France'. Semi-double lilac, maroon markings on upper petals.

Mr H. Bagust of Wyck Hill Geraniums, Stow-on-the-Wold, Gloucester,
recommends the Deacon varieties for window boxes. They give an abundance
of flowers while the size of the plants can be easily controlled.

The 'Deacon' strain is a cross between a miniature geranium and an ivy-leaf.
Here is a list of Deacon varieties:

'Deacon Bonanza'. Rose pink.
'Coral Reef'. Coral pink.
'Fireball'. Fire red.
'Lilac Mist'. Pale powder pink with deeper flushes.
'Mandarin'. Pure orange.
'Romance'. Neon purple.

Meanwhile, D. Gamble of Highfield Nurseries, Longford, Derbyshire, has
presented us with lovely 'Kathleen Gamble', a single salmon pink free-flowering

99

and of compact habit, and 'Kathleen's seedling', a crimson seedling with well-zoned foilage.

'Highfield's Comet', another Gamble variety, which was bred to replace 'Paul Crampel', is similar in colour to the veteran, but with a more compact habit and more flowers.

The Caledonian Nurseries, Bapchild, Sittingbourne, Kent, suggest:

'Emily Sylvia'. Double pink ivy-leaf. Improvement on 'Madame Crousse'.

'Galilee'. The well-known double pink so successful in London boxes.

'La France'. A beautiful double: purple uppers, petals feathered white and purple.

'Lilac Gem'. Fully double pale mauve ivy-leaf; dark scented leaf. Short jointed.

'Millfield Gem'. Pale mauve hybrid ivy-leaved type. Exceedingly good outdoor variety.

'Fragrans'. Silver-green foliage; sweet-scented.

'Lady Plymouth'. One of the desirable strongly-scented variegated varieties; cream and green foliage.

crispum variegatum. Pale lavender flowers; cream and green foliage; sweet-scented.

'Salmon Beauty.' Orient red; double; good grower and compact.

Petunia. Half-hardy summer-flowering perennial best treated as an annual. Single large-flowering hybrids, doubles, dwarfs; purples, pinks and whites. Plant early June, about 9 in. apart in turfy loam not too rich and a sunny, warm position. Large varieties, frilled and new doubles recommended. Some varieties:

'Alderman'. Indigo-violet.

'Blue Bedder'. Deep blue.

'Comanche'. Rich scarlet; robust and outstanding.

'Rose of Heaven'. Bright pink.

'Scarlet Bedder'.

Primula. A large and lovely family that includes the primrose, the cowslip, the polyanthus and many glories of marsh and woodland. They are spring-flowering perennials in various colours. *P. auricula*, *P. denticulata*, *P. vulgaris*, and the hybrid polyanthus most suited to the window-box. Plant early spring or autumn, in good loam. Propagation: division after flowering, or spring or autumn. Partial shade and constant moisture.

P. auricula. 'Dusty Miller.' There are two groups, Shows and Alpines, in various colours. 8 in. Give them a mixture of turfy loam and leaf-mould and a sprinkling of sand. Top dress in spring. Position: semi-shade. Varieties:

'Antonio'. Gold green. Strong flowerer.
'Patriot'. Well shaped, grey edged.
'White Wings'. Or if preferred White Ensign.
'Old Gold'. Lovely colour and shape.
'Bookham Star'. Fine yellow self.

Unnamed seedlings are cheaper than the named varieties and give good results.

P. denticulata. Globular head of lilac, purple, carmine, or white blossom. 12 in. March–April.

P. 'Juliana'. These look like coloured primroses. 5 in. March–April. Good varieties:

'Gloria'. Crimson. Golden eye. Beautiful.
'Kinlough Beauty'. Primrose; orange eye.
'Jewel'. Crimson.
'Wanda'. Claret. Widely grown.

The polyanthus. This great favourite is a cross between the primrose and the cowslip. 8 in. March–April. Many colours and styles. The new pinks and blues have immense stems, trusses, and stamina. Blackmore & Langdon and the Pacific Strains are magnificent. Easy from seed.

Unfortunately the flowers are adored by the sparrows and sometimes ravaged by greenfly.

P. vulgaris. The primrose. 4–6 in. March–April. It has some coloured forms, such as *P. v. coerulea*, the blue primrose.

Double Primrose. The modest double primrose is not easy, but very lovely. Worth a place in the permanent box. Two fine varieties are 'Old Mauve' and 'Old White'.

Rose. The popular miniatures, 10–12 in. tall, suit the window box: they are grafted on to understocks, are usually available in 7 in. pots. They should be planted when the rose is dormant, in medium loam 18 in. apart. A southerly aspect is essential for full success.

Pruning should be confined to trimming, cutting back flower shoots to half lengths as the flowers fade. Water liberally in summer and feed occasionally with Liquinure. Feeding should stop at the end of July: late growth will not have time to mature before the frost.

Gregory's of Nottingham now grow 100,000 miniatures a year. They are an excellent subject for the suggested second tray.

Mrs Walter Gregory names her choice for window boxes: they are compact in habit, resistant to disease and of good form and colour:

'Baby Darling'. Shades of pink and orange.
'Darling Flame'. Brilliant orange vermilion.
'Easter Morn'. Cream.
'Gold Coin'. Buttercup yellow.
'Mudy Fischer'. Bright rose pink with undertones of gold.
'Lavender Lace'. Soft lavender.
'Scarlet Gem'. Scarlet.
'Starina'. Vermillion.
'Toy Clown'. White with red or pinks edges.
'Yellow Doll'. Yellow.

Saxifraga. Perennial. A large genus of great diversity. The mossy section is very suitable for a window box but prefers shade. A collection of these makes an interesting pattern. Plant in spring or autumn: ordinary good loam and efficient drainage. Propagation: division March–April. Selections:

'Cebennensis'. Dwarf white. 4 in.
'Dubarry.' Bright red. 9 in.
'Peter Pan'. Crimson. 5 in.
'James Brenner'. Large white. 10 in.
'Sir Douglas Haig'. A large-flowered crimson. 10 in.

S. umbrosa, or London Pride, a plant that has performed such magnificent service to the city gardener, belongs to this family. No plant has more to offer; it will flower away on a pile of clinkers and in the most unpromising of window boxes. There is also *S. u. primuloides*, 'Elliott's Variety', rose pink, 8 in., a miniature form of London Pride. 'Variegata,' a useful variegated foliage variety, is now also available.

Sedum. Perennial. Various colours. May–August. Plant spring or autumn: good sandy loam, not rich. Propagation: by division in spring or autumn. Spring divisions in sandy compost will make fast headway. Looks after itself but must have full sun. Good species are:

S. acre. Yellow. The well-known stonecrop; will grow on a wall or in a gravel path. 3 in. June.

S. dasyphyllum. Blue-grey foliage; sprays white-pink flowers. Great charm. 2 in. June–July.
S. rupestre. Yellow. 6 in. May–June.
S. spectabile. Large, pink, flat, composite heads that attract the butterflies. 15 in. August–October.

Sempervivum. The house-leek. A succulent-leaved perennial. Green, glaucous, and purple rosettes. Colours various. Plant in spring or autumn in well-drained loamy soil. Enjoys sun and limited diet. Propagation is easy by breaking off the rosettes in spring or summer and planting in sandy soil. Selected species:

S. arachnoideum. Pink-red flower; red-tinted rosettes cob-webbed with white filament. 3 in. June–July.
S. a. stansfieldii. Rose red; rosettes heavily cobwebbed. 3 in. June–July.
S. tectorum rubrum. Red rosettes, pink flowers. 6–8 in. May–June.

Viola and pansy. Perennials. 6–8 in. Young stock is better than old plants. Plant April or September in rich loam with humus content. Propagation by cuttings or division in autumn. The pansy is more satisfactory grown from seed unless the plant is outstanding. Partial shade or sun will suit provided the roots are kept cool and moist. Dead-heading, feeding, and regular watering are vital. They are greedy and thirsty.

Viola Varieties:

'Chantryland'. Apricot yellow, tinged orange.
V. gracilis, 'Black Knight'. Black velvet. Award of Merit 1923.
'Jackanapes'. Brown and gold; delightful miniature with small pricked ears.
'Lorna'. Mauve-blue. Good.

Pansy Varieties: The pansy has a dark blotch in the centre of its flat face and a band of paler colour round the edges; the viola is without these markings.

'Cardinal Giant'. Bright red.
'Celestial Queen'. Sky-blue.
'Orange King'. Orange and apricot.

'Reid's New Century' Scented Pansies are superb. The Felix strain, with strange whiskered faces, have their fans. The winter-flowering pansies are an asset to the permanent box. 'Golden Sunny Boy' goes well with 'Azure Blue'.

16 *Hanging Baskets*

After the Second World War, gardeners looked upon hanging baskets as a reactionary form of gardening, and they went out of fashion. But gay and decorative, as they are, they have made a big come-back and are now even favoured by the local authorities.

Types of basket. There are several types of hanging baskets; the wooden or wire patterns can be bought at the ironmonger's or the sundriesman's. There are pot or bowl shapes, besides a series of curved fancies. The wooden baskets are to be had in all sizes, but it should be remembered that large ones, when filled with soil and plants, are heavy to handle and hang. The size of the basket should perhaps be determined by the strength of the gardener's muscles. An 18-in. basket is a serviceable size.

Soil. A good mixture of medium loam, not too light, leaf-mould, peat and sand is suitable for basket work. The container should first be lined with tightly-packed, moist sphagnum moss, followed by a layer of loam fibre, obtainable from the florist, before the earth is introduced. Care should be taken that no openings are left permitting soil to escape.

Planting. The plants should be put in firmly and at least 1 in. left between the soil surface and the rim of the basket, for watering. After planting, the basket should be immersed in water and allowed to soak, then lifted out and drained off before hanging. Some gardeners prefer to fill their baskets with pot plants and then to camouflage them extensively with moss. This method makes it easy to replace a faded or unsatisfactory plant; the spaces between the pots should be tightly packed with moss.

Water very important. The baskets should be kept in a cool airy place and watered sparingly until full root action is evident. Soon after this they will be ready for display.

Baskets dry rapidly when exposed either to the sun or the wind, and the gardener must see to it that the soil is never allowed to dry out and cake. A saucer filled with water at the bottom of the basket is essential and often a

Marigolds,
nasturtiums
and
ivy-leafed
geraniums

Violas
and
anemone

5 Geraniu[m]
in a
concrete
tub

6 Agapant[hus]
(African
Lily)

life-saver. It is a good plan to take the container down once a week and to soak it in water for a quarter of an hour and then drain it off before hanging it up again. The plants will benefit by being syringed each evening in the hot weather, even if the soil does not need watering.

Designs. I like hanging baskets, particularly of white marguerites, which have a gaiety of their own. They create an atmosphere of the South of France or the well-dressed musical comedy and fine weather.

There are two main styles of design. The arrangement can either be built up high in the centre with tall plants such as fuchsias or begonias surrounded by edging or 'trailers'; or the basket can be filled in a uniform manner, with such plants as ivy-leaved pelargoniums and petunias. The following list will suggest many associations.

A choice of plants

The choice is a wide one, for many plants will grow in this manner. Only a few are suggested here; but most window box plants grow fairly well in hanging baskets and there is, therefore, no need to give an exhaustive list.

A number of plants have surprised me by making quite good basket adornments, but few beat our old friend the nasturtium. Don't miss 'Cherry Rose.'

Centre plants

Coleus. Only suitable if the position is not windy.

Heliotrope

Ferns only if out of sun)

Marguerite

Fuchsia

Nepeta (catmint), trailing species

Verbena

Trailers and edgings

Asparagus sprengeri. With hanging fronds.

Begonia. There are several pendulous varieties in good colours which are particularly suitable for hanging baskets provided they are not exposed to the full sun:

'Beth'; salmon pink.
'Blanche'; white.
'Broadacre'; deep rose.
'Dawn'; buff yellow.
'Eunice'; light pink.
'Golden Shower'; deep yellow.

'Joan'; salmon-orange.
'Norman'; crimson.
'Rosamund'; rose pink.
'Scarlet Glow'; fiery scarlet.
'Stella'; red.

Note: Named varieties are no more expensive.

Campanula isophylla. Rather tender.

Cereus flagelliformis. The rat's tail cactus from Peru. Cacti enjoy a summer blow on a sunny window-sill.

Fuchsia procumbens. Small yellow flowers that appear during the summer and are followed by magenta-crimson berries.

F. pendula. 'Pillar of Gold' or 'Mrs Marshall'.

Helxine soleirolii. From Corsica. 3 in. Delightful.

Linaria cymbalaria. Small lilac flowers; ivy-shaped leaves. This toadflax, a hardy plant, is ideal for hanging baskets, being of a pleasant trailing habit. Seeds may be sown in pots in the spring and the seedlings transplanted into the basket. 'Sapphire', with long stems covered with dark blue white-eyed flowers, is a good 'doer'. There is a series of new and suitable trailing varieties.

Lotus peliorrchynchus. An interesting plant with a scarlet pea-like flower: a trefoil sun-worshipper.

Lysimachia nummularia. Creeping jenny: green and gold varieties. A hardy perennial. The flower stems should be cut back in April and the plant kept moist throughout the summer.

Mesembryanthemum. The Livingstone daisy is said to possess over a thousand species. It is a brilliantly coloured annual. There are pinks, yellows, and apricots. Only a few inches in height, the plant is a rapid spreader if given a well-drained soil and plenty of sunshine. Will not flower in shade.

Mimulus. Musk; one of the few that prefers the shade and moisture.

Nasturtium. One of the best and foolproof plants for hanging baskets. Seed should be sown in April. 'Tom Thumb' and 'Golden Gem' are suitable varieties; the beautiful double scented variety 'Hermann Gnashoff' should be included.

Nepeta mussinii. Catmint. Likes the sun and can be divided up from October onwards until the spring. But do not cut down until spring.

Othonna crassifolia. The African yellow ragwort that requires a sandy loam and the sunshine.

Pelargonium. The geranium, the 'King of the bedding plants', is also a perfect subject for a hanging basket. The popular ivy-leaf varieties 'Madame Crousse', and the deeper pinks 'Charles Turner' and 'Madame Thibaut', are especially suitable.

Saxifraga sarmentosa. Mother of Thousands, or Strawberry Begonia. Always reliable.

Sedum sarmentosum. Variegated foliage, pink stems, green and white leaves, and a drooping habit.

S. sieboldii. White and green foliage.

Selaginella uncinata. Creeping and moss-like. This plant should be watered copiously or syringed throughout the summer.

Zebrina pendula. The Wandering Jew, often called Tradescantia. The variety tricolor needs the sun if the green, red and white leaves are to maintain their colour. This plant is inclined to grow leggy and must be discreetly pinched back into shape. Trailers can also be pegged back into the side of the basket with a paperclip or hairpin.

17   Climbers

The town gardener often overlooks the climbing plants, but they are a boon where ground space is limited. They will decorate a wall, scramble and tumble over ugly objects, or just fall in with the gardener's design. Climbers can be planted in tubs, pots, window boxes or in any other container with a drainage hole, varying according to the character of the plant. Pots are best for the annuals and tubs more suitable for the larger woody climbers.

If the plant is to be grown against the wall, the roots should be placed at least 8 in. away from it, and the plant then gently leaned in at a comfortable angle. If it is put in tight up against a wall, the porous bricks will rob it of moisture during the hot weather, and it will be deprived of the full benefit of the rain. There are special galvanised wall pins, with soft bendable strips, obtainable at the ironmonger's, that make it possible to train the climber in the desired way. It is here that the landlord comes into the picture; the wall pins are apt to chip and loosen the pointing.

Soil and planting. Climbers like a deep-dug, well-drained, and rich soil; they need good substantial food to produce the rapid and extensive growth.

Planting can be done either in the spring or autumn. Climbers are best bought as healthy pot plants; the root ball being less disturbed by the move than when dug out of the ground.

Support. It is a waste of time to attempt to persuade a climber to change its manner of growth. It cannot, even if it would. Maybe it will cling by rootlets and be self-supporting like the ivy or be a twister like the vine. But some are without gripping power at all and utterly dependent, as is the jasmine. Some form of 'host' or support has to be provided.

There is the wooden or wire trellis available in all heights and sizes. This trellis can be made at home with $\frac{1}{2}$-in. cross-pieces. Tarred twine netting can be recommended as being flexible, mobile and cheap. The simpler and more mobile the scaffolding the better. A good new material is plastic-covered chain-link; easy to fix on wall or fence.

The plant should not be degraded by being shackled at each joint. The real climbers manage to look after themselves, the semi-climbers with neither tendrils nor adhesive discs require a helping hand. Don't wait until a plant is permanently damaged before rendering assistance.

Pruning. Veteran gardeners tell me that there has been a tendency in the past to over-prune climbers; cutting back must be judicious and performed with care, and the habit of the plant considered before snippers are sought. It is important to ascertain whether the plant flowers on the old or the young wood; a knowledge of the plant is essential before taking action, as there is the obvious danger of removing the coming season's bloom. Advice on pruning will be found under the different headings of the plants mentioned.

The climber should be kept in good shape and its growth limited to its allotted space; old and worn-out wood must be removed. The novice is warned not to prune until the spring growth breaks, so that he may be quite clear which are the live and which the dead stems. A further danger of pruning early is that it encourages young growth susceptible to frost.

Broadly speaking the majority of climbers are best dealt with after flowering; several wise town gardeners of my acquaintance boast that they manage practically without the knife, merely pinching their plants into shape when the growth is soft and young, and rubbing out the unwanted buds.

Some climbing plants and wall subjects

Celastrus orbiculatus. The Staff-vine or climbing Bitter-sweet. Beautiful twining climber as vigorous as the Russian vine, reaching a height of 40 ft, yellow autumn foliage; scarlet seeds borne by female plants.

Plant October–March. Prune weak shoots and tips of main shoots in February. Propagate by layers of young shoots in autumn or spring. Ordinary soil. Position: walls fences, or squalid places better unseen.

Chaenomeles. This is the showy ornamental quince with red, salmon, pink or white flowers from February–June, formerly called *Cydonia*, or by a popular quirk 'japonica'.

Plant in the autumn in light rich loam. The plant, not a true climber, may be trained against the wall or trellis during December. Unwanted growth and crossing branches should be cut out, and lateral shoots shortened if desired. Propagate by layering in August or September or by cuttings during July or August. It does well in any wall, even a cold north one.

C. japonica alpina. Brick-red flowers followed by yellow fragrant fruit. Very fine. In the open ground it grows 3 ft high by 8 ft wide.

C. speciosa. This is what most people have in mind when they speak of 'japonica'. It has suffered many official changes of name. Some of its best varieties are:

'Knaphill Scarlet'. Salmon; inclined to be a slow grower. 7 ft.

'Apple Blossom' (or 'Moerloosii'). Apple-blossom flowers of great charm. 12ft.

'Nivalis'. Pure white. 10 ft.

Clematis. A hardy climber. Purple, mauve, pink or white flowers in spring or summer.

Plant in March or September in well-drained loam enriched with decayed manure and a good sprinkling of old mortar or chalk.

The 'Jackmanii' and 'Viticella' sections that I recommend to the city gardener should be pruned back in February to 5 or 6 in. above the first joint made the previous season. The small-flowering section (the montanas) flower on the old ripened wood; they should be cut back after flowering and kept in shape and within bounds. Some nurserymen maintain that all newly planted clematis should be cut back in the spring to about 9 in. above the ground; others support the view that pruning should not be undertaken until the clematis is established. I suggest that the novice should wait until the second year after planting before using the knife, and that he waits to prune until spring growth has begun so that it is clear which stems are alive and which are dead.

A cool root run is one the clematis's chief requirements and can be provided by planting a small protective shrub in the neighbourhood of its roots; or a large stone will suffice to keep the sun off the lower part of the stem and the roots. Meanwhile the plant likes to see the sun and is content with a north, south or west aspect. A mulch with well-rotted manure should be an annual autumn event. Pot plants are advised.

I remember seeing *Clematis vitalba*, Old Man's Beard, cloaking the Somerset hedgerows in silver grey, revelling in the wild and undisturbed environment.

Species and Varieties

C. jackmanni. Dark violet. July–October.

C. j. superba. Slightly more intense in colour. July–October.

'Ernest Markham'. Red. June–October.

'Lady Betty Balfour'. Violet, yellow centred. August–October.

C. montana. White star flowers that bloom in profusion. May.

C. m. rubens. The deep pink form. May.

Forsythia. Deciduous shrub, with yellow flowers in late March.

Plant October–February in ordinary soil. Prune after flowering. Propagate by layering or hardwood cuttings during September. The forsythia presents no difficulties. I have seen *F. suspensa* nobly scaling a north wall.

Hedera (Ivy). Planting can be done in spring or autumn, in ordinary soil with an addition of mortar rubble.

I always suggest planting in the early autumn so that the plants have time to become acclimatised before the bad weather starts.

Ivies are excellent for furnishing the box through the winter, and even if they do get a trifle shabby towards the end of the year, they take on a new lease of life when fresh spring leaves appear.

They should be pruned in April, when old leaves and straggling shoots should be removed.

Cuttings may be taken in September or November. Common ivy is a tough and insidious plant accustomed to rough treatment. Unless well snubbed, it is likely to become the garden octopus. It is grateful for ordinary fare and will rapidly cover a wall, trellis, stump or any other object. The dusty and dull leaves repay syringing during the summer. It used to be difficult to be nice about the ivy but with the new varieties that have arrived we should reappraise the family.

Ivies can be economical if treated as ground cover inter-planted with bulbs in the spring and with geraniums, fuchsias and summer bedding in late May or early June.

Here are a few of the many:

Canariensis variegata. Leaves dark green at centre, merging to silver-grey bordered with white.

Helix 'Adam'. Small silver leaf: bushy habit.

'Buttercup'. Small leaves, new foliage bright golden yellow.

'Chicago'. Green leaves, classic shape.

'Chicago Variegated'. Green and cream-white leaves.

'Cristata'. Pale green twisted and crimped leaves tinged copper at edge in the winter.

'Glacier'. Pale green leaves margined silver.

'Goldheart'. A German variety originally known as 'Jubilee'. Small leaves with deep gold centre and dark green edge.

'Harald'. Silver and green marbled leaved.

'Lutzii'. Light gold leaved marbled and blotched green.

'Très Coupé'. A compact-growing miniature ivy with green leaves. A useful ground cover ivy for box or basket.

Ipomoea (see p. 97).

Jasminum. Climbing and trailing plants, some flowering in summer and some in winter.

Plant in spring or autumn in equal parts of loam, leaf-mould and peat. Prune after flowering, cutting back the shoots that have flowered. If the plant has grown out of hand, it must be severely cut back in the early spring. Propagate by cuttings from September to December or by layering in the summer months. When regularly syringed, the foliage remains clean and healthy throughout the summer.

Summer varieties, white-flowered, are:

J. officinale. Star-like and deliciously fragrant. One of the easiest climbers to grow.

J. o. 'Grandiflorum'. A larger form.

The popular winter-flowering jasmine with golden bells is *J. nudiflorum.* Prune moderately after flowering. As much can be done by training the jasmine in the way it should grow as by pruning it. This plant does not like to be tied too tightly. It seems to do particularly well against a west wall. It is cheering to see it bright and gay during the most trying months of winter.

Lapageria rosea (*Chilean bell flower*). Half-hardy evergreen climber with red, pink, and white wax-like flowers in summer. Exquisite but demanding generous treatment. Normally a greenhouse plant, but practical outdoors in mild districts.

Plant in February or March in equal parts of peat and loam with an addition of charcoal. Prune lightly in March, largely confining it to removing weak and sickly growth. Propagate by layering during the spring or autumn: only the strongest shoots should be attempted, and an attractive sandy peat provided for the layer.

This plant flourishes against a west wall. It is a target for slugs.

Lonicera (Honeysuckle). Hardy and half-hardy erect and twining shrubs, with cream, yellow or orange-scarlet flowers from June–September.

Plant in October or April in rich ordinary soil. *L. fragrantissima* should be pruned into shape in late spring. Other varieties are best trimmed after flowering. Propagate by strong 7 or 8 in. cuttings in July or August with the protection of a preserving jar.

A sunny position on a south or west wall is desirable; it is said that the honeysuckle thrives best when not in the close proximity of other plants and shrubs.

L. fragrantissima. Fragrant creamy white. Winter flowering.

L. japonica halliana. Evergreen variety witn cream flowers that change to biscuit. It should be cut back in the spring.

L. tragophylla. Bright yellow. Slow grower, rather showy, but, alas, unscented.

Passiflora (Passion-flower). Half-hardy climbing plant with crimson, white, and purple flowers in summer. For milder counties.

Plant at the end of March in ordinary soil enriched with well-decayed manure. Prune in February, shortening the plant to 3 ft and snubbing the short shoots to 4 or 5 in. Propagate by young shoot cuttings from April to September and layering your shoots during the summer.

The passion flower is not a hardy subject and is happier on a wall than on a trellis. The warm bricks help to ripen the wood and to strengthen it against winter conditions. A south or south-west aspect is essential.

The plant may be freely watered during the spring and summer, and a monthly stimulant of manure given throughout the growing period.

The passion flower takes a long winter rest, when it must be left in peace with its base protected by straw, bracken or matting.

Few gardeners, I fear, have been fortunate in growing this climber in a window box; having made several attempts, they have found the average life of the plant in these conditions to be short – two years at most.

The hardiest and best-known species is *P. caerulea*. Blue, and very beautiful; orange, egg-shaped fruit (if you are lucky). Its variety, 'Constance Elliott', is a charming white, seldom seen.

Polygonum. A rampant and hardy climber with creamy-white spires of blossom from July–October. Almost as extensively grown as the ivy.

Plant in spring or autumn in ordinary soil. Hard and merciless pruning is needed in the spring; unless controlled this climber becomes a veritable menace, breaking down any trellis or support with its abundance and weight. Propagate by cuttings in the spring or autumn.

This plant will look after itself. Some city gardeners will find it useful. Strangling all before it, the polygonum is capable of reaching rare heights in a single season. The difficulty in towns is to give it a suitable host; it is a twiner, not a clinger.

Species

P. baldschuanicum. Quick and rampant, cream flowers. Common.

P. aubertii. More distinguished. Pink.

P. multiflorum. Pink.

Rose. Those who have no open garden have only a limited scope for growing roses, but some of the climbers will make a fair show in large tubs. Ramblers on walls are likely to trap all the mildew for miles around.

Plant in spring or autumn in loam enriched with decayed manure. Prune at the end of March or in early April, when weak wood should be removed and side shoots shortened. Old flowering shoots may be cut back after flowering. Propagate by cuttings in September or November or layerings in September or October, or by budding in July. It is important that the rose's roots should be spread out when planted, and that they should be planted firmly. A rose fertiliser may be given once a week when the buds form, until after flowering. Young basal shoots are encouraged by watering the base of the climber; a bucket of soapy water will stimulate new virile growth and will help to reduce the insect population.

No flower can hope to be as popular as the rose but unfortunately it dislikes confinement and the draughty conditions that so often go with a tub. However, a climber will frequently survive where the bush has given up the struggle.

I have found the veteran buff-salmon variety 'Gloire de Dijon' willing to grow on a north wall. And of course you can't go wrong with 'Paul's Scarlet' or the single, golden Mermaid or the red 'Allen Chandler'. Meanwhile, few can compete with the romantic beauty of pink 'Madame Gregoire Staechlin' with crimson buds.

Mr S. M. Gault, for many years Superintendent of Regent's Park and the famous Queen Mary Rose Garden, has given me this choice for town climbers:

'Danse de Feu'. Vivid scarlet.
'Dortmund'. Crimson with a white eye, rather like 'American Pillar', but flowering for a longer period.
'Golden Showers'. Always in bloom.
'Handel'. Cream and pink.
'Joseph's Coat'. Yellow, orange and red.
'Maigold'. Bronze-yellow, semi-double.
'Pink Perpetue'. A gorgeous pink.
'Sander's White'. Scented.

Virginia creepers. Another genus that has been plagued by changes of name. Formerly called *Vitis* or *Ampelopsis*, they are now to be found in up-to-date catalogues under the attractive name of *Parthenocissus* (meaning 'Virgin Ivy'). Hardy, deciduous self-clingers, for any large wall. Plant in spring or autumn in any good ordinary soil.

Species

P. henryana (Vitis henryana). The most beautiful. On a sunless wall the dark-green leaves become handsomely variegated. In autumn a brilliant red.

P. thomsonii (Vitis thomsonii). Young growths claret. Autumn shades of crimson and red. Very fine.

P. tricuspidata (Ampelopsis veitchii and *Vitis inconstans)*. The commonest and most vigorous sort.

P. quinquefolia (Vitis quinquefolia). The true Virginia Creeper from America. Much prettier than the foregoing but equally vigorous.

Wistaria. Deciduous climbing shrub with mauve or white flowers in May and June.

Plant in March or April in rich sandy loam. Train carefully until there is a good framework. Prevent it from twining round itself. Then in summer pinch back the side shoots to 4 or 5 leaves and in winter prune back to 2 in. of the base of the shoot. This promotes free flowering.

The wistaria prefers a southern aspect sheltered from the cold wind. Pot plants should be bought when possible as this plant is sometimes exceedingly slow in settling down. The usual species grown is *W. sinensis*.

Other climbers. I have already given the climbers more than their fair share of space, believing as I do that they have been rather overlooked by the city gardener. But there are others I should just like to mention: the ceanothus and the cotoneaster that can be trained to climb 10 ft although not true climbers, the loganberry, the less stereotyped morello cherry that will grow in the shade, and the brewery-smelling hop (quite a pleasant scent) that will climb up a greasy pole when properly established. The golden hop is a wonderful climber.

Annual climbers. There are several annual climbers that cover a considerable amount of ground in one season. They include the sweet pea, and purple *Cobaea scandens*, a delightful perennial best grown as an annual, the multi-coloured convolvulus, *Ipomoea*, or morning glory (see p. 97), orange scarlet *Eccremocarpus scaber*, although not a true hardy annual, linaria and the nasturtiums, including the canary creeper. Seed should be planted in the ordinary way when all danger of frost is over. Strong country seedlings usually have a pull over the plants grown in the city.

I should like the gardener to give a thought to the sweet potato; planted in the springtime 3 in. deep it will flower in August: also to the scarlet runner, the last vegetable of the season, that will brighten up an area or any dull place during the summer with its gay orange sprays, even if it does not perceptibly increase food production. It should be sown in May about 2 in. deep.

The introduction of two new beans, pink 'Sunset' and white 'Achievement', will increase the demand for these climbers. Planted at either end of the box and given a string or trellis support they will be found most rewarding.

18 Tubs

Many a city-dweller has the necessary ground space for a tub: a back yard, a veranda, or the back or front doorstep will suffice. Unless the tub is on legs, it should, whenever possible, be stood on bricks. Tubs make very nice Christmas presents.

The cube Versailles cuisses seen outside the large French Château or some of our stately homes such as Merriworth Castle, Maidstone, hold veteran orange trees.

These dignified containers, with side panels that slot in and out, are practical: in many cases two sides can be removed, and the tired soil rubbed away to make place for fresh and stimulating compost. This treatment enables an orange tree to survive for decade after decade.

Should the shrub's growth be too exuberant, two sides of the tub can be be removed and some of the roots pruned in early spring.

Tubs can also be grand containers, obtained from a nurseryman, in teak or oak; they can also be home-made out of a packing case, a converted wash-tub or a beer barrel. A rhubarb or seakale pot, turned upside down and crocked with large slabs of slate, will serve the same purpose, while Italian oil-jars make attractive containers for a veranda.

Wooden tubs are best in hot sunny positions; the evaporation of moisture is not as rapid as in earthenware tubs. They can, of course, be of any size, but resident shrubs usually require a container of 16 or 18 in. diameter.

There are now also to be had some reasonably priced tubs or urns in fine-grade concrete ('reconstituted stone') of good design and there are the new fibre-glass urns and tanks, not cheap.

Recipe for a beer barrel

Some gardeners remove one end of a beer barrel and cut a number of 6–8 in. apertures in the side of the barrel in which to place the plants.

The apertures should not be made lower than 2 ft from the barrel's base; the gardener can make as many openings as he pleases but two floors are advised for the small-sized barrel, and in the large barrel three floors should not be exceeded. The openings should alternate regularly storey by storey so that those on the first floor are directly beneath those on the third floor.

The drainage system is similar to that of the window box. Half a dozen drainage holes should be cut or burnt in the bottom of the barrel and the inside of the container stuffed with newspapers and charred, or the wood may be treated with horticultural Cuprinol.

Planting can then be begun with about a 6-in. foundation of crocks followed by a layer of soil roughage. As the openings are reached the plants should be inserted. A few lumps of charcoal added to the compost will help to keep it sweet, and if the plants are packed in with moss the soil is not so easily washed away by watering.

The top should be planted with the larger plants, and the tub will be found a perfect container for aubrietas and the dianthus family. Different-shaded varieties of aubrietia grown on the various storeys are effective, but any small plants, particularly those of trailing habit, will look well.

This tub with its many apertures requires constant and regular watering when the plants are in active growth.

A cement yard or walk may get red hot on a sunny summer day: blocks on the corners of the container, that lift the tub sufficiently to allow the air to circulate below it, will spare the roots from burning.

Culture

It is important to start off with a good soil mixture; and the summary on soil already given for window boxes in Chapter 2 applies to tubs.

After the shrub or plant has been in the tub for two or three years, much of the nourishment will have been taken from the soil; this threatens starvation and involves re-planting with fresh compost. The operation must be undertaken either in the spring or autumn, but not in the height of the summer.

Top dressing is necessary once or twice a year, when the tired surface soil should be removed and replaced with a good loam and leaf-mould mixture. Any reputable proprietary organic fertiliser can then be applied but must be used strictly according to the directions. Two spring dressings may be considered necessary, with a month's interval between the applications.

Soot water and liquid manure are helpful to the plant about to flower. Plants, like people, welcome a change of food.

Water may be freely given. The gardener can drive a thick stick deep down into the centre of the tub before planting; when the stick is removed the passage may be used for watering. This channel will serve throughout the summer; after watering the stick can be replaced. If the plants are thirsty customers, any porous tube can be inserted and used to water the lowest row of plants.

Tubs should be kept on the dry side throughout the winter; dry roots are less vulnerable to frost than wet ones.

A small shrub in a large tub seldom thrives: it is a mistake to give it more soil than it needs.

Matching tubs and boxes

Some gardeners prefer to have their tubs and window-boxes to match; this is quite simple, as everything grown in a window box will grow equally well in a tub. When there are a number of windows and tubs and an attractive colour scheme, the result is most effective.

I still remember vividly a house in Kensington Palace Gardens just before the war, with quite a dozen windows and a generous number of immense tubs all decked with large, striped, purple-and-white petunias. It was a great sight.

Then there was a back yard in Chelsea with two window boxes full of pink-mauve stocks and a tub bulging with white heavily-scented *Lilium regale*.

Whether the gardener decides on flowers to match or flowers that contrast, he can have, if he so wishes, the two or three seasonal plantings in the same order as the window box gardener: spring bulbs, summer bedders and an autumn show, as well as his shrubs.

What to grow

Almost anything, and certainly everything that will grow in the window box. The seasonal programmes and colour schemes given for window boxes will also serve for tubs. The suggestions that follow are a medley illustrating briefly the qualities of a few suitable subjects and their special tastes, if any. It is by no means a complete list, but we may specially note that, with due care in watering, the tub allows us to grow some of our finest shrubs.

Strawberries – a speciality. The return after a hundred years of the fashion of growing strawberries in barrels has created a great deal of interest. Any robust barrel that has not been creosoted will do and 2-in. apertures should be made as explained earlier in this chapter.

The introduction of a perforated zinc tube run down to 2 in. above the bottom row of plants seems the most efficient way of getting water down to the plants.

By this method the gardener will be able to plant twenty-seven strawberries – twenty-three through the holes and four in the top of the barrel. With any luck he will be spared birds and slugs.

Runners potted in June or July will fruit well their first season. Place the barrel in an open position. Mulch with manure in March. Remove runners when they appear. The strawberries may be left undisturbed for three years.

Varieties. It is difficult to beat Royal Sovereign. Several long-fruiting 'remontant' autumn fruiting varieties are now on the market, which are ideal for the box.

TREES AND SHRUBS

Acer. The maple, a hardy deciduous tree. Plant in autumn or spring in well-drained loam. It likes leaf-mould and will grow in partial shade.

Species

A. japonicum. Also its golden and finely cut varieties.
A. palmatum. Also its varieties yellow and scarlet tinted.

The Japanese maples are small, easy growing, and brightly coloured: yellow, bronze, red, purple, silver and all shades of green. Decorative for eight months of the year. Expensive at outset but a good buy.

Camellia. This is an evergreen that calls for a sheltered place, against a south or north wall safe out of the wind or in a protected veranda. It prefers the South of England.

Plant in March or April in equal parts turfy loam peat and sand. Water moderately only from September–March and copiously afterwards. Prune only when necessary: this should be done in March. Winter protection during a hard winter is helpful.

Species and Varieties

C. japonica 'Alba Simplex'. Pure white single with golden anthers.
C. j. elegans. An old favourite. Large, peony-centred flowers. Often known as *Chandleri* 'Elegans'.
C. j. 'Imbricata Rubra'. A double dark red. Compact and upright growth.

Chaenomeles (Japanese Quince). See previous chapter. A wall is not necessary.

Erica (Heather). Hardy evergreen flowering shrub with pink, purple, red, and white flowers.

Plant in October or March in sandy peat. All but the winter-flowering heathers and one or two others need a lime-free soil. All like the sun. Prune back in April or immediately after flowering.

Varieties (a few only):

E. hybrida 'Dawn'. A dwarf with large deep pink elongated bells, that flowers from June to October.

E. vagans 'Mrs D. F. Maxwell'. Spikes of cerise flowers from July onwards.

For winter: *E. hybrida* 'George Rendall'; *E. carnea* 'King George', 'Queen Mary', 'Vivellii', and 'Springwood White'.

Hydrangea. Hardy deciduous flowering shrub, with panicles of paper-like pink, blue or white flowers from July to September.

Plant in February or March in 2 parts rich loam (which must be free of lime if you want blue flowers), 1 part well-decayed manure and sharp sand. Water freely between March and October. Very old wood should be cut out after flowering in order to make room for the new growth that will bear the next season's blossom. Otherwise, no pruning is necessary. Plants showing flower benefit when given liquid manure.

This is an amenable town plant, tolerant of the shade, and easily increased in the spring by cuttings. The flower of some varieties can be 'blued' by watering with aluminium sulphate obtainable at the florist's. If there is a heavy lime content in the soil the flowers will resist this treatment. Good blue-ers are: 'Goliath', 'Maréchal Foch', 'Parsifal', 'Vicomtesse de Vibraye', and the beautiful Lacecap 'Blue Wave'.

Lavender. Hardy flowering shrub with mauve, purple, pink, and white flowers in summer. Easy in any soil. Trim into shape after flowering.

Species and varieties

Lavendula spica. Grey-blue; the old English lavender; $2\frac{1}{2}$ ft.

L. spica 'Munstead'. Rich colour, probably the best all-round dwarf lavender; 15 in.

L. spica nana atropurpurea. 'Hidcote' variety; deep purple. One of the best, 2 ft.

L. spica 'Vera'. Grey-blue; habit dense and spreading; 2 ft. Form *nana alba* is white.

The white lavender that is rarely seen and the new forms are no more difficult to grow than the familiar blue. There is also a pale pink variety. A mixture of all three colours planted together can be quite effective.

Magnolia. Few flowers can compare with the beauty and perfect shape of the magnolia. Plant in autumn or early spring in 2 parts sandy loam, 1 part peat or leaf-mould and sand.

A large tub, at least 21 in, in diameter, is required. Water freely in summer, moderately at other times. The plant often suffers a setback when moved. No lover of lime. A large terrace, rather than a small space is best for these lovely shrubs.

Species and varieties

M. soulangiana. The best-known magnolia with spreading branches and white flowers stained rose-purple at the base. April–May.

M. s. 'Rubra'. The flowers are deeper in colour.

M. stellata. White star-like flowers. March–April. Profuse.

Rhododendron. I look upon the rhododendron as one of the best tub plants. If the tubs are filled with acid soil, the rhododendron-lover on chalk will still have the opportunity of growing this plant.

Plant any time between the end of September and the middle of April in one-third peat, one-third lime-free loam, one-third sand with a 4-in. potful of hoof and horn meal to each barrowful of soil.

The soil should be well firmed up with a rammer as the rhododendron is planted. The tub should not be filled too full, so that a generous margin is allowed for watering. Water copiously in dry weather. Mulch with decayed manure in May. Remove seed pods directly the flowers fade by snapping off the cluster.

Warning!

To water the rhododendron or other chalk-hating plants with tap water of a high lime content is to sign their death certificate.

Varieties. Four good 'doers' are: 'Bagshot Ruby', ruby-red; 'Cynthia', rosy-crimson; 'Mrs Holford', deep salmon; and the well-known 'Pink Pearl'.

The famous rhododendron nursery, Waterers and Sons, recommend the following plants for tubs:

Large-flowered varieties: 'Britannia', red; 'Corona', pink; 'Doncaster', dark red; and 'Souvenir de Dr S. Endtz', rose.

Small-flowered varieties: 'Waterer's Hybridum', rose; and 'Blue Diamond', blue.

Standards look extremely well in tubs, but the gardener must see that their roots are mulched and not sun-baked.

Here are five bright, well-known varieties that will serve this purpose:

'Doncaster'. Bright crimson and compact.

'Mrs G. W. Leak'. Pink with brown-purple blotch is my favourite rhododendron.

'Pink Pearl'. A famous pink, large flower and truss.

'Purple Splendour', Dark purple with deeper blotch.

'Sappho'. White blotched maroon.

A young *Ponticum* rhododendron seedling is often a free gift in a peat district, where it grows rampant. Planted in a barrel in acid soil, its mauve flowers would strike a cheerful note in a drab back yard.

Rose. In addition to the climbers and the miniatures, dealt with previously, some hybrid teas and floribundas may be grown in tubs. See previous chapter.

Special care should be taken when planting roses. The roots should be unravelled and spread out about 5 in. below the surface of the soil, and the bushes planted firmly. Pruning may be done at the end of March or early April and unsatisfactory shoots shortened to dormant buds 3–9 in. from the base. A rose fertiliser should be given once a week from the time buds form until the flowers open. If the plants are syringed with insecticide from early May, there should be no serious trouble with greenfly. City roses appear to be attacked early in the season.

Bush roses fare reasonably well in tubs, but few survive more than two years of confinement. I have seen 'Phyllis Gold', the pure rich yellow hybrid tea rose, flowering handsomely in a tub after four years' residence. However, this unfortunately, is not her constant habit.

Specialists now offer small collections of roses suitable for town growing. Autumn flowering is encouraged by cutting back summer-flowering shoots after the blooms fade.

Mr Harry Wheatcroft has given me his pick of roses for tubs:

Hybrid Teas: 'E. H. Morse', red; 'Bettina', orange; and golden-yellow 'Sunblest'.

Floribundas: salmon pink 'Tip Top', fragrant, dwarf and bushy; and 'Topsi', brilliant orange-red, winner of the Royal National Rose Society's Trophy and Gold Medal 1972.

Mr S. M. Gault recommends:

Hybrid Teas:

'Alec's Red'. Exhibition blooms, good scent.

'Fragrant Cloud'. Geranium red, strongly scented.

'Mischief'. Coral salmon.
'Mullard Jubilee'. Deep pink, shapely and scented.
'Pink Favourite'. Rose pink, disease resistant.

Floribundas:

'City of Leeds'. Deep salmon.
'Escapade'. Rosy-magenta, semi-double (one of Jack Harkness's favourites).
'Kerryman'. Pale pink with deeper coloured edges.
'Pernille Poulsen'. Salmon, early flowerer.
'Pink Parfait'. Pink with yellow base.
'Vera Dalton'. Clear pink.

Hybrid musk shrub:

'Ballerina'. Apple blossom pink with a charming white eye, recurrent flowering and a good tub plant.

Rosemary. Hardy evergreen shrub with purple-mauve flowers in spring, but seldom flowers in the city. Give some protection in very cold winters.

Plant in April–May in ordinary soil with an addition of mortar rubble. Rosemaries require watering freely throughout the summer. Shoots (not the old wood) should be cut back after flowering (or in early summer if there is no flower) and the plant checked from sprawling.

Selections

Rosmarinus officinalis. Also its trailing varieties.
'Miss Jessop's Upright'. Fine habit for tub work.

The sweet-scented rosemary with its charming grey foliage and sentimental history has no liking for a polluted atmosphere. Its behaviour in industrial towns is uncertain.

Sweet Verbena. Deciduous shrub, rather tender, with unimportant lilac flowers in August, but grown for the refreshing odour of its foliage, which gives it its popular name of Lemon-scented Verbena. Plant in March in 2 parts loam, 2 parts leaf-mould and sand.

This plant requires a sheltered position in full sun near a south wall and a little protection in the winter; an old sack will do, but care must be taken that it is not removed too early or young shoots may be nipped by an unexpected frost. Shoots may be pruned to within an inch of the base in February or March.

Ask for *Lippia citriodora*.

Yew. Hardy evergreen tree, botanically called *Taxus baccata*.

Plant in September–November or February–May in ordinary soil with a good leaf-mould content.

The Romans started the gentle art of topiary, cutting trees and shrubs into ornamental designs, often in the shape of animals. It is a fascinating craft, and it will be found that the yew submits to the constant use of secateurs without injury.

You can either buy your ready-trained plant and go the easy but rather expensive way, just keeping the pattern or animal in good shape. It will need constant checking in the summer months once it has settled down. Or you can start from scratch with a strong young yew and train your corkscrew or teddy bear for yourself. Mulch well every year, as these plants are gross feeders. You should visit a nursery and pick out a plant that will lend itself to your design. It is wise to begin modestly with a globe or pyramid and to move on to the more ambitious shapes such as dogs, squirrels, birds, and arm-chairs. Shaping is best done in April. It is important not to let the yew get altogether dried out and the soil caked during the summer.

This is not a back-bending occupation and requires more thought than muscle. It can become a family affair – for you, your children and grandchildren.

A cut box or yew, as a shape, a bear or small beast, gives a friendly look on the doorstep either side of the door.

Other candidates. A host of other woody plants come to my mind as I close this list: *Caryopteris clandonensis*, a delightful blue autumn-flowering shrub of about 2½ ft; *Ceratostigma willmottianum*, another blue-flowering charmer; the buddleias with their showy spikes of purple or mauve bloom; the Persian lilacs, the cotoneasters, the ribes or flowering currants or twin standards of the stately bay.

Mr. J. L. Russell, an expert on shrubs, reminds me of four others: *Escallonia* 'Donard Seedling', a South African evergreen that loves the seaside and has pale pink flowers that turn to white; *Potentilla farreri*, a dwarf with bright yellow flowers that appear from May to September; *Pyracantha atalantioides* (with red berries) *P. rogersiana flava*, brilliant with golden-yellow berries in the autumn; and *Viburnum burkwoodii* with its sweet-scented white-tinted pink flowers that arrive in April.

Perhaps it should be pointed out that the escallonia and pyracantha need a stake support until they have established themselves.

BULBS AND CORMS IN TUBS

Tubs are excellent containers for bulbs. Hyacinths, narcissi or tulips planted close together give a wonderful display; the hyacinths and narcissi look their best when all of a kind, but the double tulips mixed, in all gay colours, are dazzling.

Small bulbs – the crocus, grape hyacinths and chionodoxa – planted as a carpet liven up dull evergreens and deciduous shrubs.

Lily. No flower, in my opinion, surpasses the scent, beauty and charm of the lily. They look very fine indeed in tubs.

Plant about 6 in. apart from October to February, in practice when the bulbs are available. *L. candidum* should be planted in August or September. Soil: a well-decayed leaf-mould with a sprinkling of sand. This may be drawn in around the plant as it develops.

Top dress in spring with leaf-mould or decomposed cow manure, obtainable from the lily-grower. Liquid manure may be given during the flowering period. Lilies should not be moved unless they are overcrowded or in bad health.

Varieties

L. candidum. The Madonna or Bourbon lily; white, summer. 4–5 ft. The bulbs should be planted shallow, and only just covered with soil.

L. regale. White, gold, and rose-purple. July, 3–6 ft. Plant 6 in. deep.

L. umbellatum. Red. June, 5 ft. Planting depth 6 in. There are several striking umbellatum varieties, among them 'Golden Fleece', golden yellow tinged scarlet, 2 ft, and 'Orange King', 3 ft, a true and glowing orange.

L. 'Enchantment'. Flame-red. 4 ft. Splendid. Plant 4 in. deep.

Gladiolus. The Primulinus, Miniature, and Butterfly varieties are better for tubs than the large-flowering gladiolus, being shorter and presenting less petal surface to the wind. Any of the fairly tall 15–18 in. hardy and half-hardy annuals can be used to carpet the tub and will take away the naked appearance of the bottom half of the gladiolus spike.

Plant in March or April, 4 in. deep, 5 or 6 in. apart, in good loam enriched with manure.

Mr Charles Unwin, the gladiolus expert, suggests the light, graceful and reasonably cheap *G. primulinus* hybrids in mixture. Most of them are well under 3 ft.

He adds three lovely miniatures:
'Bo Beep'. Apricot-salmon.
'Greenbird'. Greenish-sulphur.
'Zenith'. Rich shell-pink.

Culture. Fortnightly doses of liquid manure are beneficial when the buds form. Corms may be lifted in November, the shrivelled outworn corms removed from the new ones, and then laid out to dry off in some frost-proof place.

Gardeners might like to try *Gladiolus murielae*, the Acidanthera or Scented Gladiolus from Abyssinia in their tub. It looks like a gladiolus but has the delicious scent of a fragrant tuberose. White with deep maroon blotch. 2 ft 6 in. Plant early May.

Herbaceous Perennials for Tubs

Acanthus. A perennial with purple and white spikes that possesses great architectural merit; rather tender; flowering from June–August.

Plant in spring or autumn in sandy loam, in the sun or partial shade; it has no particular requirements but dislikes the damp.

The acanthus is a magnificent perennial with noble foliage and classical appearance which the Greeks used largely in their decorative designs. I have seen this plant flowering profusely, with grand 3½-ft spikes of white and purple, in a garden in Kensington Square.

Agapanthus. An evergreen, almost hardy, with blue, or white, flower spikes of 30–36 in. in July. Often called 'African Lily'.

Plant in autumn in heavy loam. Give light protection during a hard winter. If regularly top dressed, can be left in the same tub for a number of years. Will require to be watered freely during the summer, and a weekly dose of liquid manure in the spring will improve the summer flowers. Flowers best when well established.

The African china-blue lily is one of the best-known tub plants. The smaller, and probably more hardy, white species is less seen.

Fuchsia. (See page 97.) A sub-shrub of perennial habit.

Hosta (Syn. **Funkia**). A hardy perennial with pale or deep lilac or white flowers from July to September.

Plant in spring or autumn in good loam with an addition of well-decayed manure. It thrives best in partial shade.

Species

H. fortunei. Glaucous blue leaves.
H. japonica albo-marginata. Green leaves edged with white.
H. ovata aurea. Yellow-green leaves.

Dr Funk, a German botanist, introduced this accommodating plant. The plantain lily will look after itself and is ideal for the tub in the shade and the gardener who is not always in attendance.

The pale lilac one-sided sprays of bloom are rather insignificant, but the leaves are striking. The *Funkia* is a very desirable and easy-going foliage plant.

Iris. Previous chapters have been concerned mainly with the bulbous irises, but the lordly Bearded Iris, a hardy perennial, can be grown in tubs. They flower in May and June in wonderful colours.

Plant directly after flowering in ordinary soil with an addition of lime or mortar rubble. The modern 'bearded flag' iris is magnificent and easy to grow. It does not like manure, and the rhizomes, which are not roots but thickened stems, must be planted horizontally and only partially covered. At least half of the rhizome should remain above the surface of the soil.

It is easy to propagate by division of rhizomes in the spring, autumn or after flowering. The plants should be divided every three or four years, and the untidy sword-like leaves can be cut back to within 6 in. of the base after transplanting. A top dressing of superphosphates and sulphate of potash in early May and perhaps a taste of bonemeal in February will provide flowers of quality. The tubs should be in full sun.

The iris is the most popular town plant because of its adaptability and modest demands upon the time and skill of the gardener. Now that the flowering period has been so greatly extended, the complaint of the shortness of the iris's flowering season is no longer justified.

Perhaps I should say that the old blue flag that consents to flower anywhere is unique in this. The newcomers, among them the pinks and reds, are more particular. Iris can be successfully interplanted with gladiolus.

Mr George Whitelegg suggests the following varieties for tubs:

'Aline'. Azure-blue self. 3 ft.
'Blue Ensign'. Blue self. Free. 2½ ft.
'Cherie'. Flamingo-pink ruffled flowers, tangerine beard. 2½ ft.
'Corrida'. Sky-blue self. 3 ft.
'Golden Hind'. Buttercup yellow. Orange beard. 3 ft.

I should like to put in a good word for the black iris, which are particularly glamorous. Among them 'Black Banner', silky blue-black, 'Black Forest' and velvety 'Sable'. Planted with clear pink 'Airy Dream', they are bound to please.

Perhaps reddish-crimson 'Ethel Peckham' should be mentioned because she is scented. Lovely, but, alas, short flowering.

Lupin. A perennial of various colours flowering in May and June. Plant in October or April in sandy loam. On no account use any manure or lime.

Cut down the spikes (not leaves) after flowering. The lupin requires about $2\frac{1}{2}$–3 ft to display itself at its best. Weekly doses of a balanced fertiliser given before the flowering season will improve the spikes of bloom. The lupin is happy either in the sun or partial shade.

The lupin has been vastly improved during the last years by means of cross-breeding, selection and the skill of Mr George Russell. The city gardener should try some of the cheaper unnamed seedlings of the better varieties that are no more difficult to grow than the exhausted blue. The new and remarkable combinations of colours that have recently appeared do not appeal to every-body, but there are perfect selfs that deserve notice.

Lupins should be replaced at least every two years as they invariably go downhill; their untidiness in late summer should be graciously forborne, and the stems not severely cut back until the autumn.

The following are not too tall and are free-flowering:

'Blushing Bride'. Cream to palest pink; one of the toughest.
'Canary Bird'.
'Fantasy'. Yellow and terracotta.
'Guardsman'. The best of the orange-reds.
'Lady Diana Abdy'. White and blue.
'Lady Fayre'. Deep pink; strong grower.
'Wheatsheaf'. Golden-corn.

Why not have a bit of fun and grow a few from seed? It's quite easy even in a tub but avoid lime in your soil. I suggest your trying the new strain lupin 'Lulu' mixed not yet to be had in separate colours: it is dwarfer (about 2 ft), sturdier and neater than its predecessors.

Vinca. The perennial periwinkle with China blue flowers from June onwards.

Plant in spring or autumn in fibrous loam with a decayed manure content. It has no cultural fads and is as easy as pie. Useful for flourishing in a completely sunless corner. Species and varieties:

V. major. Large blue flowers.
V. m. 'Variegata'. Silver-marked leaves.
V. minor 'Aureovariegata'. Golden-marked leaves.
V. minor 'Bowles Variety'. Large azure flowers.

The periwinkles serve as ground cover to other plants since they are low growing. There are also purple, white, and pink varieties.

Yucca. An evergreen perennial with large, creamy-white bells in spikes 30 in. high in October or April, with large leaves and a tropical air.

Plant in July to August in ordinary well-drained soil. It will put up with almost anything other than damp. Cut the flower spike down to the ground after blooming.

Varieties:

Y. filamentosa. Cream.
Y. flaccida. Cream. Free flowering.
Y. gloriosa. Cream. Upright habit.

Adam's Needle or the Mound Lily, as the *Yucca* is called, will grow in a tub as a permanent feature; that is, if you care to cultivate the prickly thing. It likes the sun, and light protection during a hard winter. The *Yucca* is an acquired taste.

Other tub plants. I give also a list of city-growing perennials in addition to those already given (see p. 43). This second list adds those considered too tall for window-boxes.

	Colour	Height	Flowering Time
Althaea (Hollyhock)	Various	6–9 ft	Aug.–Sept.
Aquilegia (Columbine)	Various	1½–2½ ft	May–June
Aster (Michaelmas Daisy)	Various	2½–3 ft	Aug.–Oct.
Chrysanthemum	Various	2–4 ft	Aug.–Oct.
Campanula lactiflora	White, blue	4 ft	June–July
Delphinium	Blue, purple	3–5 ft	July–Aug.
Digitalis (Foxglove)	Purple, pink	3 ft	July–Aug.
Echinops (Hedgehog Flower)	Blue	3 ft	July–Aug.
Kniphofia (Poker Plant)	Red-orange (and a white newcomer)	3–5 ft	Aug.–Sept.
Oenothera (Evening Primrose)	Yellow	1½ ft	June–Aug.
Paeonia (Paeony)	Pink, red	2½ ft	May–June
Papaver (Poppy)	Various	3 ft	June–July
Phlox	Various	2½–3 ft	Aug.–Sept.
Trollius (Globe Flower)	Yellow-orange	2–3 ft	May–June

The bedding plants and annuals all grow well in tubs. Dahlia, geranium, nasturtium, nicotiana and lobelia can be specially recommended. The China aster is a great standby, and seedlings are usually plentiful. Nasturtiums are best when mixed with sturdy plants, otherwise they have a habit of flinging themselves about. In addition to the window-list, the taller perennial asters and chrysanthemums can be used in the tubs. They flower in September. Here are some of them:

Aster: Novi-Belgii Section

'Lassie'. Clear soft-pink. 3½ ft.
'Apple Blossom'. Delicate pink; 3–3½ ft.
'Chequers'. Purple; 2½ ft.
'Marie Ballard'. Clear blue; 3 ft.
'Winston Churchill'. Beetroot-purple; 2¼ ft.
'White Swan'. Clear white; good tub plant.

Border Chrysanthemum

'Arnhem'. Orange-bronze; 3 ft.
'Carefree'. Chestnut with a gold reverse; 3 ft.
'Imperial Yellow'. Deep yellow double; 40 in.
'Ladybower'. Rich pink; 3 ft.

19 *Water-Lilies in Tubs*

Small concrete tanks or tubs, or any form of tub receptacle that will hold water, of about 6 in. or 12 in. depth, with 8–12 in. of good heavy loam, will make a happy home for a water lily. The tubs may be sunk into the ground up to their rim. A sunny position should be chosen.

Plant any time from March–July. Re-pot every third year in April or May, using a rich, turfy loam with a sprinkling of coarse bonemeal. Two that I like are:

> *Nymphaea pygmaea alba.* The small white Chinese species, the baby of the family, often grown in decorative bowls with only a few inches of water. Flowers in profusion throughout summer.
> *N. p. helvola.* Sulphur-yellow form with mottled foliage.

Mr Reginald Perry, who is the kingpin on water-lilies and aquatic plants, has kindly chosen six for the small tub and advised me on their culture.

White

> *N. odorata minor.* Star-shaped and scented.
> *N. tetragona alba.* The smallest water-lily. Abundant foliage. Needs only a few inches of water.

Pink

> *Laydekeri lilacea.* Free flowering.
> 'Firecrest'. Rich pink, orange stamens tipped red. Good for cutting. A larger variety.

Crimson and Red

> *Laydekeri fulgens.* Crimson-carmine. Clusters of orange-red stamens.
> *L. purpurata.* Wine red. One of the finest for tubs.

For the ambitious gardener willing to introduce a couple of rocks into his container, there is a wide range of marginal plants. Mr Perry chooses these:

Butomus umbellatus. The flowering rush and the most beautiful of our native aquatics. Rose flowers. 3 ft.
Caltha palustris. The Marsh Marigold. Yellow. Spring. 1½ ft. Or any member of the caltha group.
Iris. Any of the water iris other than the *pseudacorus.*
Mimulus ringens. Lavender blue. Dark green foliage. 1½ ft.
Pontederia cordata. The Pickerel Weed. Lovely blue. Not unlike a small delphinium with handsome heart-shaped leaves. 2 ft.
Typha minima. Shiny green grass-like foliage. Heads of brown inflorescence. 1½ ft. Erroneously referred to as the 'bulrush'.

Culture. The depth of water need only be 6 in. for the smaller growing species. The lily should be planted firmly into the medium on the base of the tub. At least two underwater oxygenating plants are needed, such as *Callitriche autumnalis,* one of the few submerged aquatics that are active during the winter months, and *Tillaea recurva.*

After planting, the water will become clear but will turn brown or green in a few days and remain so until the plants have settled down. Gardeners *must not* drain away the water when it becomes discoloured. Patience, please! Once the lilies begin to grow and the oxygenating plants establish themselves, all will be well.

Now all that have to be added are a couple of fish: shubunkins, golden orfe or our old friend the goldfish. Lastly, add half a dozen *Planorbis corneus,* the ramshorn snail, the best known of the race and an energetic scavenger.

The prettiest tubs I have seen were in Copenhagen in the spring. They were planted with young, slim silver birches. There were yellow trollius with the brightest of blue forget-me-nots at their feet.

Good luck to your boxes, baskets and tubs; may you, in gardener's language, succeed even to the rooting of a monkey's tail.

Window Box Suppliers

Barbican Florists
2 The Podium
London Wall
London, EC2

J. R. Barralets
Pitshanger Lane
Ealing
London, W5

Clifton Nurseries
Clifton Villas
Warwick Avenue
London, W9

Longmans Ltd
154 Fenchurch Street
London, EC2

Moyses Stevens
99 Cheapside
London, EC2
Berkeley Square
London, W1

Rassells
80 Earls Court Road
London, W8

Joshua Upton Ltd
5 Egerton Terrace
London, SW3

Verine Products
Folly Faunts House
Goldhanger
Maldon
Essex

Windowflowers Ltd
Staines Road Nurseries
Feltham
Middlesex

Index

Table of approximate metric equivalents

½ in.	1·3 cm	9 in.	23 cm
1 in.	2·5 cm	10 in.	25 cm
2 in.	5 cm	11 in.	28 cm
3 in.	7·6 cm	12 in.	30·5 cm
4 in.	10 cm	18 in.	45·7 cm
5 in.	12·7 cm	24 in.	61 cm
6 in.	15 cm	36 in.	915 cm
7 in.	17·8 cm	48 in.	1·22 m
8 in.	20 cm	60 in.	1·5 m